Come, Follow Jesus!

(the real Jesus)

www.ComeFollowJesus.net

David A. Reed

This book is dedicated to Katy Tripp,
who asked me to write a book
about following Jesus

September, 2011

www.ComeFollowJesus.net

Books by David A. Reed include:
Jehovah's Witnesses Answered Verse by Verse
Mormons Answered Verse by Verse
Parallel Gospels in Harmony - with Study Guide

Come, Follow Jesus! (the real Jesus)

ISBN 1450575021

EAN-13   9781450575027

Scripture References

Unless otherwise noted, Scripture quoted in this book is from the World English Bible, a copyright-free translation in the public domain.
LB   The Living Bible © 1971 by Tyndale House Publishers
NASB   New American Standard Bible © 1995 by Lockman Foundation
NCV   The Holy Bible, New Century Version © 2005 by Thomas Nelson, Inc.
NEB   New English Bible © 1961, 1970 by Oxford University Press and Cambridge University Press
NIV   The Holy Bible, New International Version © 1973, 1978, 1984 by International Bible Society
NKJV   New King James Version, Holy Bible © 1983 by Thomas Nelson, Inc.
RSV   Revised Standard Version © 1946, 1952 by Division of Christian Education of the Churches of Christ in the United States of America

Contents

Who needs to follow Jesus?

Are you at the end of your rope, caught up in a web of troubles with no way to escape?

Jesus has rescued countless people in similar circumstances. He can help you.

Are you living comfortably but wondering what life is all about and where it will all end?

Our Creator sent Jesus to reveal the meaning of life and our eternal purpose.

Have you lost faith in hypocritical religious leaders?

Stop following them, and follow Jesus instead.

Are you disturbed by the terrible things happening in the world today?

The Bible says such events would occur just before Jesus returns in power.

Have you been hurt by those you trusted in for leadership and guidance and help?

Turn to Jesus for healing and help. He won't disappoint you.

Does it make sense to you that a lifetime of learning and growing should simply end at the grave?

Jesus rose from the grave to give his followers everlasting life.

Has your church abandoned the Bible's teachings?

This, too, was predicted in the Bible, but God will judge false teachers.

Do you fear that your sins have cut you off from God?

God sent his Son to take your punishment on himself and free you from sin.

Have you planned for next year, and for retirement, but not for eternity?

Learn what Jesus reveals about your eternal future.

Actually EVERYONE needs to follow Jesus, because,

as detailed in the Bible, the God who created heaven and earth sent Jesus to teach us how to live and to grant us forgiveness for failing to live that way in the past—and will soon send Jesus again with great power to rescue his followers and wage a final war against this wicked world that rejects the Bible's message.

Jesus said: "Come, follow me."

—Luke 18:22

"'Come to me, all you who labor and are heavily burdened, and I will give you rest.

"'Take my yoke upon you, and learn from me, for I am gentle and lowly in heart; and you will find rest for your souls.

"'For my yoke is easy, and my burden is light.'" —Matthew 11:28-30

"'My sheep hear my voice, and I know them, and they follow me. I give eternal life to them. They will never perish, and no one will snatch them out of my hand.'" —John 10:27-28

Jesus of Nazareth lived 2000 years ago in the Middle East. He preached in ancient Jerusalem and the surrounding regions inhabited today by Israelis and Palestinians. Religious leaders were angry when Jesus exposed their hypocrisy, and jealous when he drew crowds of followers, so they falsely accused him of crimes and turned him over to the secular authorities for execution—a cruel death by crucifixion—unknowingly fulfilling ancient prophecies about how the promised Messiah or Christ would die a sacrificial death to take away our sins and give his followers eternal life. But hundreds of eye-witnesses testified that Jesus rose from the dead. Before ascending to heaven, he promised to return, this time with great power, to replace human governments with the Kingdom of God. In the meantime, he would remain with us, invisibly. Appearing alive to eleven of his followers after rising from dead, Jesus said to them:

"'All power in heaven and on earth is given to me. So go and make followers of all people in the world. Baptize them in the name of the Father and the Son and the Holy Spirit. Teach them to obey everything that I have taught you, and I will be with you always, even until the end of this age.'" —Matthew 28:18-20 NCV

Obeying this command, Jesus' followers wrote down the things he taught, and the things that he did—healing people of all sorts of diseases, and even raising the dead to life—and they preached that message to others, first in Jerusalem, then throughout the Mediterranean area, and to the ends of the earth. We have their testimony about Jesus and his teachings preserved for us today in the books of the New Testament in the Bible.

Jesus' invitation to "Come, follow me" is still open. He instructed his original followers to "go and make followers of all people in the world." And besides praying for those original followers, Jesus also prayed to his heavenly Father for future followers saying, "My prayer is not for them alone. I pray also for those who will believe in me through their message." (John 17:20 NIV)

So, the invitation is open to you. Jesus invites YOU to become his follower.

How can you do that? What is involved in following Jesus?

As we just read above, people today can become followers of Jesus by believing in him through the teaching of his original followers—the ones who wrote the Gospels and the New Testament in the Bible. Jesus commanded those original followers to teach future followers "to obey everything that I have taught you." (Matt. 28:20 NCV) So, following Jesus today involves believing in him and obeying the things he taught his original followers, as found in the Scriptures they wrote.

If you ask people today what it means to follow Jesus, you will hear many different contradictory answers to that question. But the only correct answer is the answer found in the pages of the Bible where Jesus' teachings are actually written down for anyone to read.

So, in order to follow Jesus, you need to read the Bible yourself, or to listen to someone reading it out loud—the entire Bible, verse after verse and chapter after chapter, not just isolated passages quoted out of context or included as part of someone else's discussion.

What about just joining a church and listening to what the pastor preaches on Sunday mornings? Won't that make you a follower of Jesus? Even though they quote from it, most churches today no longer preach the Bible. Many preach directly contrary to what the Bible says on important matters. And many others preach only part of what the Bible says—just the parts that are popular and that don't offend anyone. As Jesus' early follower the Apostle Paul warned,

"...the time will come when people will not listen to the true teaching but will find many more teachers who please them by saying the things they want to hear." —2 Timothy 4:3 NCV

Paul warned that already in his day some churches accepted false teachers preaching another Jesus, a Jesus different from the real Jesus:

"You are very patient with anyone who comes to you and preaches a different Jesus from the one we preached. You are very willing to accept a spirit or gospel that is different from the Spirit and Good News you received from us." —2 Corinthians 11:4

This same thing has been happening for centuries, with the result that there are many millions of people today who think they are following Jesus, or who say they are following him, but who are not following the real Jesus at all.

Jesus knew ahead of time that things would turn out this way. He warned:

"'Not every one who says to me, "Lord, Lord," shall enter the kingdom of heaven, but he who does the will of my Father who is in heaven. On that day many will say to me, "Lord, Lord, did we not prophesy in your name, and cast out demons in your name, and do many mighty works in your name?" And then will I declare to them, "I never knew you; depart from me, you evildoers."'"

—Matthew 7:21-23 RSV

The Apostles and other early followers of Jesus faithfully preached the message he had taught them, and they recorded this message in their writings that now make up the Bible's New Testament. But, even at that time there were portions of the Christian message that were unpopular and that people did not want to hear. For example, when the Apostle Paul shared the Gospel message with Roman governor Felix, the governor listened gladly to the part about putting faith in Christ, but he did not want to hear the part about the lifestyle Jesus commanded his followers to live, and about God's coming judgment:

"He listened to Paul talk about believing in Christ Jesus. But Felix became afraid when Paul spoke about living right, self-control, and the time when God will judge the world. He said, 'Go away now. When I have more time, I will call for you.'" —Acts 24:24-25 NCV

Powerful and influential people today often behave in much the same way as governor Felix, responding favorably to appealing parts of the Gospel message, but not wanting to hear the parts about living right, self-control, and the time when God will judge the world. In so-called "Christian" countries, such people may even join a church and consider themselves to be Christian. As major financial contributors, or as people who do a lot of the work in the church, they may tell the pastor they don't want to hear him preach on certain topics that they find offensive, or that they think might offend others in the audience. The Apostle Paul faithfully preached the full force of Jesus' message, even though he was jailed and eventually killed for doing so, but many church leaders over the centuries have compromised the message to please their listeners.

Likewise today, the pastor of a church may feel obliged to leave out offensive topics from his Sunday messages, in order to keep his job and to avoid losing church members. (I have heard even Bible-believing pastors of Bible-believing churches admit that they have done this—leaving out mention of money, or of certain sins, or leaving out the full force of God's judgment message—at the request of influential members of their church, or out of fear of losing their job.) When this sort of thing continues for years and then for decades, a church or denomination can end up preaching just a fraction of Jesus' message—giving listeners an unbalanced or twisted view of what it means to follow Jesus, the real Jesus of the Bible. And that is exactly what has happened.

Very often today churches that call themselves Christian preach a Jesus who loves and accepts everyone and everything, and who doesn't require anything of anyone. That is not the same Jesus who gave the command to baptize followers and to teach them "to obey everything that I have taught." (Matt. 28:20 NCV) That is not the same risen Jesus who sent this message to the Christian church in the city of Thyatira:

"'I know what you do. I know about your love, your faith, your service, and your patience. I know that you are doing more now than you did at first.

"'But I have this against you: You let that woman Jezebel spread false teachings. . . . by her teaching she leads my people to take part in sexual sins . . . I have given her time to change her heart and turn away from her sin, but she does not want to change. So I will throw her on a bed of suffering. . . . I will also kill her followers. Then all the churches will know that I am the One who searches hearts and minds, and I will repay each one of you for what you have done.'" —Revelation 2:19-23 NCV

Do you find that message offensive? Some people will stop reading this book right now, and toss it into the trash. Why? Because they have already chosen to follow a different Jesus—not the Jesus of the Bible who spoke the words above.

How can you know if a church or a preacher is following the real Jesus and teaching everything that he taught? Only by prayerfully reading the Bible yourself, and becoming personally familiar with its message.

The purpose of this book is to draw your attention to key passages in the Bible that will help you learn how to accept Jesus' invitation to "Come, follow me"—passages that highlight what we must do to follow Jesus, according to Jesus himself and according to his first followers.

How can you follow Jesus?

Following Jesus is the right thing to do, and the best thing we can do for ourselves and for others we love and care about. And it is the proper thing to do if we appreciate our loving Creator who has given us life and who has given us all the good things we enjoy. It is what God wants us to do. But how do we go about doing it?

When Jesus called the original disciples to follow him, it was clear how they had to do it. Peter and Andrew got out of their fishing boats and followed Jesus, literally walking after him. (Matt. 4:19-20) Matthew got up from his tax-collecting desk and followed Jesus, literally walking after him. (Matt. 9:9) But how can we today follow Jesus?

We cannot see him and physically get up from our seat and follow after him as he walks down the road. But we can believe that he died for our sins, that he rose from the dead, that he is alive today, and that he accepts people as his followers now just as he did back in the first century. Jesus is not visible to us, but that does not stop him from hearing our prayers and answering them.

So, if you tell Jesus right now that you are sorry for your past sins, and that you want to leave them behind and begin a new life by following him, he will hear you and will forgive your sins and will accept you as his follower.

"'I will never turn away anyone who comes to me.'"

—John 6:37 Today's English Version

Although he is not visible to us, Jesus promised his followers:

"'I am with you always, even to the end of the age.'" —Matthew 28:20

When you become his follower, Jesus comes to live with you and in you by means of his Spirit—God's Holy Spirit:

"'One who has my commandments, and keeps them, that person is one who loves me. One who loves me will be loved by my Father, and I will love him, and will reveal myself to him. . . . If a man loves me, he will keep my word. My Father will love him, and we will come to him, and make our home with him.'" —John 14:21, 23

So, we today can come into a personal relationship with Jesus that is just as real as what the first followers experienced when they got up from their seats and followed Jesus down the road. We can ask him questions as they did, even though we can't see him. And we can listen to his replies as we prayerfully read his teachings in the pages of the Bible.

In some ways our relationship with Jesus today can be even closer than what the first disciples experienced when they could see Jesus and share meals with him. That is because everyone who puts faith in the risen Christ is "born again" spiritually as a child of God. Jesus explained it this way:

"'I tell you the truth, no-one can see the kingdom of God unless he is born again. . . . I tell you the truth, no-one can enter the kingdom of God unless he is born of water and the Spirit. Flesh gives birth to flesh, but the Spirit gives birth to spirit. You should not be surprised at my saying, "You must be born again."'"

—John 3:3-7 NIV

We are born again when we trust in Jesus to save us from our sins and commit ourselves to obey him. God then adopts us as his children, sending his Holy Spirit into our hearts:

"To prove that you are sons, God has sent into our hearts the Spirit of his Son, crying 'Abba! Father!'" —Galatians 4:6 NEB

("Abba" was a term Jewish children used when addressing their human father, and a term Jesus himself used when addressing his heavenly Father. See Mark 14:36.)

In some way that is beyond our understanding, Jesus actually comes to live with us and in us when we believe in him and choose to follow him. Yes, it is beyond human understanding, and that is why the Apostle Paul refers to it as

"this mystery, which is Christ in you" —Colossians 1:27 NIV

It really is a mystery—beyond human understanding—but the Bible assures us that Jesus actually comes to live in the hearts of his followers:

"that Christ will live in your hearts by faith" —Ephesians 3:17 NCV

Because followers of Jesus come into this close spiritual relationship with God as his adopted children, we can find super-human strength to overcome our inborn tendencies to sin, and we can look forward to eternal life:

"You, however, are controlled not by your sinful nature but by the Spirit, if the Spirit of God lives in you. And if anyone does not have the Spirit of Christ, he does not belong to Christ. But if Christ is in you . . . he who raised Christ from the dead will also give life to your mortal bodies though his Spirit, who lives in you."

—Romans 8:9-11 NIV

So, following Jesus is much more than reading about an ancient historical figure and trying to live and love the way he did. It is much more than just joining a church that was founded centuries ago by his early followers. It is a real relationship with a real live person—the risen Son of God. He invites you to come into this relationship as his follower. But it is your choice. It is up to you to open the door, to invite him into your life and into your heart:

"'Behold, I stand at the door and knock; if any one hears my voice and opens the door, I will come in to him and eat with him, and he with me.'" —Revelation 3:20 RSV

You can respond right now to Jesus' invitation to be his follower. Turn to him in prayer, and tell him that you are sorry for your sins—including the sin of ignoring God and the Bible—and that you now want to leave your sins behind and change your heart and your life by following him and obeying him. Even though he is invisible, Jesus will respond to your prayer by accepting you as his follower. He will forgive your sins and begin to lead you in the way you should go.

'But I'm a sinful person, not fit to be a follower of Jesus!'

Is that how you feel about yourself? A rough and vulgar fisherman when he encountered Jesus, the man who was to become the Apostle Peter felt the same way about himself:

"But Simon Peter . . . fell down at Jesus' knees, saying, 'Depart from me, for I am a sinful man, Lord.'" —Luke 5:8

The Apostle Paul wrote similarly about himself, even calling himself a chief or especially notorious sinner:

"I was before a blasphemer, a persecutor, and insolent. However, I obtained mercy, because I did it ignorantly in unbelief. The grace of our Lord abounded exceedingly with faith and love which is in Christ Jesus.

"The saying is faithful and worthy of all acceptance, that Christ Jesus came into the world to save sinners; of whom I am chief. However, for this cause I obtained mercy, that in me first, Jesus Christ might display all his patience, for an example of those who were going to believe in him for eternal life." —1 Timothy 1:13-16

So, if Jesus could save someone as sinful as Peter or as sinful as Paul, he can save you, no matter what your life has been like up until now. In fact, Jesus said he did not come for righteous people, but for sinners:

"'Those who are healthy have no need for a physician, but those who are sick. I came not to call the righteous, but sinners to repentance.'" —Mark 2:17

Jesus illustrated his concern for sinners by comparing himself to a shepherd who has a hundred sheep, with one that wandered away—the way a sinner wanders away from God. And he described the joy in heaven when such a lost person repents:

"'Which of you men, if you had one hundred sheep, and lost one of them, wouldn't leave the ninety-nine in the wilderness, and go after the one that was lost, until he found it? When he has found it, he carries it on his shoulders, rejoicing. When he comes home, he calls together his friends and his neighbors, saying to them, "Rejoice with me, for I have found my sheep which was lost!" I tell you that even so there will be more joy in heaven over one sinner

who repents, than over ninety-nine righteous people who need no repentance.'" —Luke 15:4-7

To drive home the point that there is great joy in heaven when a sinner repents, Jesus immediately gave another illustration concerning a woman who had ten valuable coins and lost one of them:

"'Or what woman, if she had ten drachma coins, if she lost one drachma coin, wouldn't light a lamp, sweep the house, and seek diligently until she found it? When she has found it, she calls together her friends and neighbors, saying, "Rejoice with me, for I have found the drachma which I had lost." Even so, I tell you, there is joy in the presence of the angels of God over one sinner repenting.'" —Luke 15:8-10

So, no matter how sinful you have been, God will welcome you when you change your heart and life by turning to him in repentance and deciding to follow Jesus. In fact, Jesus died to take away your sins, heal you, and give you new life:

"He himself bore our sins in his body on the tree, so that we might die to sins and live for righteousness; by his wounds you have been healed." —1 Peter 2:24 NIV

It doesn't matter how serious your sins have been. Jesus' sacrificial death on the cross will cover them. It is just as when God invited ancient Israel to repent. He told them:

"'Come now, let us reason together,' says the LORD. 'Though your sins are like scarlet, they shall be as white as snow; though they are red as crimson, they shall be like wool.'" —Isaiah 1:18

Naming very specific serious sins when writing to the church in Corinth, Greece, the Apostle Paul said that people in that church had previously practiced those sins, but were now washed clean:

"Do you not know that the wicked will not inherit the kingdom of God? Do not be deceived: Neither the sexually immoral nor idolaters nor adulterers nor male prostitutes nor homosexual offenders nor thieves nor the greedy nor drunkards nor slanderers nor swindlers will inherit the kingdom of God.

"And that is what some of you were. But you were washed, you were sanctified, you were justified in the name of the Lord Jesus Christ and by the Spirit of our God." —1 Corinthians 6:9-11 NIV

So, even people who have committed very serious sins against God can be washed clean and made acceptable to God when they repent and put faith in

Christ. This, of course, is not a license to keep on practicing sin willfully in the expectation that there will be no consequences. Rather, when Jesus healed a man, he told him to "stop sinning":

"Later Jesus found him at the temple and said to him, 'See, you are well again. Stop sinning or something worse may happen to you.'"

—John 5:14 NIV

But even Christians may fall into sin. If you have slipped and fallen after accepting Christ, you should not feel eternally condemned. God still calls you to repentance. The Apostle John wrote this to Christian believers:

"My dear children, I write this to you so that you will not sin. But if anybody does sin, we have one who speaks to the Father in our defense—Jesus Christ, the Righteous One. He is the atoning sacrifice for our sins, and not only for ours but also for the sins of the whole world."
—1 John 2:1-2 NIV

And the letters that Jesus had John write to the seven churches in Revelation, chapters 2 and 3, called on the members of five of those churches to repent:

"'Remember where you were before you fell. Change your hearts and do what you did at first.'"
—Revelation 2:5 NCV

Even toward "that woman Jezebel" in the church at Thyatira who "leads my people to take part in sexual sins and to eat food that is offered to idols," Jesus held out the opportunity for her to repent. Jesus told John to write,

"'I gave her time to repent, but she refuses to repent of her sexual immorality.'"
—Revelation 2:21

Don't be like Jezebel, who refused to repent. No matter how serious your sins, Jesus calls you to repent and turn to him for salvation, and to begin following him. There will be rejoicing in heaven. Jesus promised,

"'I will never turn away anyone who comes to me.'"

—John 6:37 Today's English Version

Your new life as a follower of Jesus

Jesus himself spelled out what people in the future would need to do to follow him. Appearing alive to his first followers after rising from the dead, Jesus said to them:

"'All power in heaven and on earth is given to me. So go and make followers of all people in the world. Baptize them in the name of the Father and the Son and the Holy Spirit. Teach them to obey everything that I have taught you, and I will be with you always, even until the end of this age.'" —Matthew 28:18-20 NCV

These instructions make it clear that we are really following Jesus when we are baptized in the manner Jesus outlined, and when we then go on to learn and to obey everything that Jesus taught.

What did Jesus teach? It would be impossible to present here a better picture of what he taught than the understanding you will gain by reading the four Gospels for yourself. So, I will not be offended at all if you now put this book aside for a while and pick up the Bible instead to read what Matthew, Mark, Luke and John wrote about Jesus' life, ministry and teachings. In fact, I would encourage you to do that.

As you read the Gospels, you will notice that Jesus started out his ministry with a call to "Repent!" This is not a familiar word for most people today, but the dictionary tells us that "repent" means to feel sorry for past conduct, to regret or be conscience-stricken about past actions and attitudes—with such sorrow as to want to change one's life for the better. This call for people to change their hearts and lives was such an important theme of Jesus' preaching that he began his work on earth with this call for people to "Repent!" and ended his work on earth with the same message.

Matthew says this about how Jesus began his ministry:

"Jesus began to preach, and to say, 'Repent!'" —Matthew 4:17

And Luke shows that Jesus concluded his ministry on earth with the same message:

"that repentance and remission of sins should be preached in his name to all the nations." —Luke 24:47

Moreover, decades later when the Gospel message had already spread throughout the Mediterranean area, resulting in the formation of many Christian churches, the risen Christ appeared to the then aged Apostle John in a vision in which Jesus commanded John to send messages to seven major Christian churches, and the messages to most of those churches included a call for their members to "Repent!"—even though they were already Christians:

To the church in the city of Ephesus, Jesus said:

". . . Repent and do the things you did at first. If you do not repent, I will come to you and remove your . . ." —Revelation 2:5 NIV

To the church in the city of Pergamum, he said:

". . . Repent therefore! Otherwise, I will soon come to you and will fight . . ." —Revelation 2:16 NIV

To the church in the city of Sardis, the risen Christ said:

". . . Remember, therefore, what you have received and heard; obey it, and repent. But if you do not wake up, I will come like a thief, and you will not know at what time I will come to you. . . ."

—Revelation 3:3 NIV

To the church in city of Laodicea, Jesus said:

". . . Those whom I love I rebuke and discipline. So, be earnest, and repent. . . ." —Revelation 3:19 NIV

(I purposely quoted just a few words from the messages to these churches—enough to show that Jesus was calling their members to repent—but you would benefit from reading these messages in their completeness in Revelation chapters 2 and 3.)

So, Jesus calls on us to "Repent!"—change our hearts and lives—when we first turn to him to as our Savior and Lord. And he repeatedly calls Christians to "Repent!" even later during our walk with him as his followers. When we regularly read the Bible and prayerfully think about the things it says and how those words apply to our lives, God's Holy Spirit shows us the changes we need to make to grow up as God's adopted children and to become more like Jesus.

When we first turn to Christ, asking him to forgive our sins and expressing our desire to follow him, we typically need to repent of major sins—to change our hearts and lives in major ways. For example, in the Apostle Paul's first letter to the church in ancient Corinth, he lists some of the sins that various members of that church used to practice before becoming followers of Jesus:

"Or don't you know that the unrighteous will not inherit the Kingdom of God? Don't be deceived. Neither the sexually immoral, nor idolaters, nor adulterers, nor male prostitutes, nor homosexuals, nor thieves, nor covetous, nor drunkards, nor slanderers, nor extortioners, will inherit the Kingdom of God.

"Such were some of you, but you were washed. But you were sanctified. But you were justified in the name of the Lord Jesus, and in the Spirit of our God." —1 Corinthians 6:9-11

If you open your Bible and read the context of this passage, you will see that Paul was reminding those in the Corinthian church that they had left these practices behind when they became followers of Jesus. But the thrust of Paul's message was that some in the church were continuing to practice these sins, or were falling back into such practices—and that this was totally unacceptable.

First Paul pointed out that some in the church "do wrong and cheat, and you do this to other believers" (1 Cor. 6:8 NCV), then he wrote the passage above, and then he went on to say, "Surely you know that your bodies are parts of Christ himself. So I must never take the parts of Christ and join them to a prostitute!" (1 Cor. 6:15 NCV) Evidently there were some in the church who either failed to abandon those sinful practices, or who were in danger of falling back into behaving badly like that.

How could that happen in the Christian church in ancient Corinth? In much the same way that it happens in churches today, when pastors and teachers fail to put the same emphasis on repentance that Jesus did. The city of Corinth was a place where bad behavior and sexual immorality were commonplace and accepted by the community, very much like our corrupt society today. So, apparently the local leadership in the church failed to rebuke and correct church members when they behaved like their non-Christian neighbors, and it became necessary for the Apostle Paul to rebuke and correct them through his letter that now forms part of our Bible. Paul was, in effect, reminding them that they had repented of their bad conduct when they became followers of Jesus, and that they needed to guard against slipping back into such bad conduct again.

Church leaders today can similarly be affected by the corrupt and sinful world that surrounds us, and can be influenced to water-down the call to repent, or even to omit it entirely from their preaching. In fact, the invitation to follow Jesus is often presented today as if it were another one of the various competing self-help or self-improvement programs offered on television, in magazines and on the internet: 'Follow Jesus, and you will be happy!' or 'Solve all your problems by following Jesus!' or something to that effect. Beautiful smiling people sit in front of the TV camera and tell how Jesus brought them happiness.

There is some truth to that: Jesus is the only way to real, lasting happiness. But that was not the main focus of Jesus' message, and not the main focus of the New Testament. As we just read above, the focus was on salvation from sins, repenting of those sins, and changing hearts and minds by learning to obey and follow Jesus. Moreover, Jesus told his early followers they would be hated and persecuted, and would suffer just as he suffered:

"'If the world hates you, keep in mind that it hated me first. If you belonged to the world, it would love you as its own. As it is, you do not belong to the world, but I have chosen you out of the world. That is why the world hates you. Remember the words I spoke to

you: "No servant is greater than his master." If they persecuted me, they will persecute you also. ' "   —John 15:18-20 NIV

"'. . . you will be arrested, persecuted, and killed. You will be hated all over the world because you are my followers.'" —Matthew 24:9 NLT

Jesus' first followers experienced this persecution and hatred in ancient Palestine and throughout the Roman Empire, and today, too, there are large areas of the earth where Christians face intense persecution, most notably in China, India, North Korea, and dozens of Muslim nations. And even in the nations of Christendom there have been long episodes when true Bible-believing Christians have been persecuted by governments and church leaders who were "Christian" in name only—such as during the Inquisition. Many observers see a new wave of persecution coming, as Western nations toss aside biblical beliefs and biblical morality, making heroes of celebrities who practice sin and sexual immorality, and making it punishable as a "hate crime" to speak out against such sins.

So, the visible benefits of following Jesus may not always outweigh the visible disadvantages—in this life, before we go to our heavenly reward. The Apostle Paul wrote that he himself had been "in prison . . . flogged . . . beaten with rods . . . stoned" and had faced many other dangers as a result of his ministry (1 Cor. 11:23-27 NIV). That is why Paul wrote,

"If only for this life we have hope in Christ, we are to be pitied more than all men."   —1 Corinthians 15:19 NIV

But our hope in Christ goes beyond this life. As Jesus said,

"'Blessed are you when people insult you, persecute you and falsely say all kinds of evil against you because of me. Rejoice and be glad, because great is your reward in heaven, for in the same way they persecuted the prophets who were before you.'"

—Matthew 5:11-12 NIV

Our persecution for following Jesus may not be violent, but we may face opposition, ridicule or contempt from friends or relatives. If our repentance from sin involves quitting certain practices or activities that we used to share with friends, those friends may react with hostility toward us and toward the Gospel message. As the Apostle Peter wrote,

"Strengthen yourselves so that you will live here on earth doing what God wants, and not the evil things people want. In the past you wasted too much time doing what nonbelievers enjoy. You were guilty of sexual sins, evil desires, drunkenness, wild and drunken parties, and hateful idol worship. Nonbelievers think it is strange that you do not do the many wild and wasteful things they do, so they insult you."   —1 Peter 4:2-4 NCV

We may encounter such verbal persecution from friends and associates, from workmates, or even from close relatives. And that may prove to be a test for us. Jesus said,

"'He who loves father or mother more than Me is not worthy of Me; and he who loves son or daughter more than Me is not worthy of Me. And he who does not take his cross and follow after Me is not worthy of Me.'" —Matthew 10:37-38 NIV

Jesus' first followers were all Jews, and they preached the message about Jesus at first to mainly Jewish audiences. For centuries Jews had heard the Old Testament read aloud each week in their synagogues, so they already knew that the true God created the world and everything in it, and they were already familiar with the Bible's history of mankind's rebellion against God. Jews already knew how God wanted people to live, because their Scriptures contained laws from God declaring what was bad and what was good. And Jews were already familiar with the passages in their Scriptures promising a coming Messiah or Christ—a savior and king appointed by God. So, it was only necessary to explain to them that Jesus was the one foretold, to provide evidence to convince them of that fact, and then to acquaint them with Jesus' life and teachings. So, to such a Jewish audience in Jerusalem, the Apostle Peter could present a brief review of Jesus' life and ministry, and then urge them to repent by turning their lives around and following Jesus:

"Peter said to them, 'Repent, and be baptized, every one of you, in the name of Jesus Christ for the forgiveness of sins, and you will receive the gift of the Holy Spirit. For the promise is to you, and to your children, and to all who are far off, even as many as the Lord our God will call to himself.' With many other words he testified, and exhorted them, saying, 'Save yourselves from this crooked generation!'" —Acts 2:38-40

Notice that Peter's call was for his listeners to "repent" or turn their lives around and follow Jesus, and that thus they would receive "forgiveness of sins"—which Jews understood because they already knew God's requirements for living right, and each one knew his or her own failure to live up to those requirements.

Back in the first century when the Apostles Peter and Paul began preaching, the Jews were the only people on earth who were in the habit of reading the Old Testament—the part of the Bible that had already been written and circulated during the centuries before Jesus was born. Most people on earth had no knowledge of the true God or his inspired Bible. The non-Jewish audiences Jesus' disciples began preaching to in Africa, Asia and Europe were descended from ancestors who had long ago abandoned and forgotten the Creator, and who had now been worshiping idols for as long as they could remember—statues of wood, stone or metal representing many different imaginary gods and goddesses. So, it was necessary to take a different approach when sharing with them the Good News about Jesus. But it was still necessary to call them to "repent."

For example, the Apostle Paul took this approach when speaking to an audience of educated and scholarly men in Athens, Greece:

"'You men of Athens, I perceive that you are very religious in all things. For as I passed along, and observed the objects of your worship, I found also an altar with this inscription: "TO AN UNKNOWN GOD." What therefore you worship in ignorance, this I announce to you.

"'The God who made the world and all things in it, he, being Lord of heaven and earth . . . made from one blood every nation of men

. . .

"'. . . we ought not to think that the Divine Nature is like gold, or silver, or stone, engraved by art and design of man. The times of ignorance therefore God overlooked. But now he commands that all people everywhere should repent, because he has appointed a day in which he will judge the world in righteousness by the man whom he has ordained; of which he has given assurance to all men, in that he has raised him from the dead.'" —Acts 17:22-31

Notice that Peter speaking to a Jewish audience and Paul speaking to non-Jews both told their listeners to "repent" in order to follow Jesus, or as the New Century Version of the Bible interprets that word, "change your hearts and lives." What sort of changes must you make when you repent and choose to follow Jesus? This book will point out some passages from Scripture that specify those changes, but in order to be sure you are obeying all the things Jesus commanded, you really need to prayerfully read the Bible for yourself. As you read, ask God for understanding, for insight, for faith to believe, and for strength to walk in his ways.

Find fellowship with other followers of Jesus

If you wish to follow Jesus, it is important to find other followers of Jesus to meet with. Jesus said that he would be personally present in gatherings of his followers, even though we cannot see him:

"'Where two or three are gathered together in my name, there I am in their midst.'" —Matthew 18:20

Christians gather together for Bible study, to share testimonies, to hear Bible-based sermons, to celebrate Communion, to support and send out missionary preachers, to help and pray for one another, and to sing songs of praise to God. The New Testament records how the Apostles and early disciples set the pattern by continuing to meet together after Jesus ascended to heaven, and how new congregations of believers sprang up in one city after another as the message about Christ spread across the ancient Roman Empire.

"Let us hold fast the confession of our hope without wavering, for he who promised is faithful; and let us consider how to stir up one another to love and good works, not neglecting to meet together, as is the habit of some, but encouraging one another, and all the more as you see the Day drawing near." —Hebrews 10:23-25 RSV

Who should you meet with? In the first century it was very clear: Jesus' followers in Jerusalem gathered together with the Apostles, and in cities around the Mediterranean Sea there were congregations founded by the Apostle Paul or other traveling missionary preachers. But now in the twenty-first century a city may have ten or twenty different churches with different names, belonging to different denominations, and separated from each other by different practices, customs and doctrines—as well as small house churches meeting in private homes. Does it matter which one you choose to attend? Which one is the true church filled with followers of the real Jesus?

The true church is not any man-made denomination or organization, but is the worldwide body of all those individuals who belong to Christ. The true church is

"the general assembly and church of the firstborn who are enrolled in heaven" —Hebrews 12:23 NASB

Once you become a follower of Jesus, you immediately and automatically become a member of that true church, and your name is registered in heaven in the true church's membership rolls. Jesus knows those who belong to him.

Then, what about all the different churches and organizations? Which one should you fellowship with? Or should you avoid the organized churches with large buildings, and instead meet with fellow believers in a private home?

Some groups will tell you that they are the one true church, and that all the others are false. Others recognize one another as fellow Christians, but maintain separate organizations due to different preferences in style of worship or different traditions for conducting baptisms, celebrating Communion, and so on—relatively minor distinctions—while agreeing with one another on the main elements of their faith.

Does it matter which one you choose to fellowship with? Yes, it matters very much. Some churches or groups calling themselves "Christian" are actually destructive cults that ruin people's lives. Some are mere social clubs. Some lead people away from Jesus, while using his name to make people feel good about doing bad—even teaching that Jesus accepts the very things he condemned.

Jesus himself warned,

"'Not every one who says to me, "Lord, Lord," shall enter the kingdom of heaven, but he who does the will of my Father who is in heaven. On that day many will say to me, "Lord, Lord, did we not prophesy in your name, and cast out demons in your name, and do many mighty works in your name?" And then will I declare to them, "I never knew you; depart from me, you evildoers."'"

—Matthew 7:21-23 RSV

And the Apostle Paul warned the elders of the church in Ephesus that leaders would arise among them who would mislead the churches:

"I know that after I leave, some people will come like wild wolves and try to destroy the flock. Also, some from your own group will rise up and twist the truth and will lead away followers after them."

—Acts 20:29-30 NCV

So, how can you discern whether a church is really doing God's will? How can you know whether those in leadership are following Jesus, or are leading away followers after themselves?

You won't be able to make complete sense of the confusing array of churches and denominations without knowing what the Bible says about the history of the early churches, and what later church history says about the how some of the original churches became corrupt, and how they broke up into various denominations and groups. Such a study could take years to complete, and your understanding of these matters may change as you grow and mature in the faith and as you gain experience in dealing with other believers. You may find yourself moving from one church or fellowship to another as you learn more, or as the fellowship you are in changes its character, which often happens as different individuals assume positions of leadership.

But none of this should cause you to postpone fellowshipping with others who want to follow Jesus. Approach the matter prayerfully, trusting that God will answer your prayer by guiding you into a fellowship where you can learn and where you can help others—even if it eventually turns out that what you learn is that you need to go elsewhere, and that you end up helping others go with you. (Compare my personal testimony found later in this book.)

Reading through the New Testament even just once will give you a general sense of what Jesus and his Apostles taught, and will allow you to compare that with what you hear in church.

Due to the widespread apostasy (departing from the faith) in Christian churches today, it is important to exercise caution when choosing a body of believers to associate with. But, at the same time, you should not look for perfection, because you won't find it. Consider, for example, the very first Christian group with Jesus and the twelve Apostles at its nucleus. If you attended their meetings, you might have noticed that one of the Apostles was embezzling funds from the group's cash account—Judas Iscariot who later betrayed Jesus. (John 12:6) But did that mean it was a phony church you should avoid? Obviously not, because Jesus himself was there, leading the group. Likewise today, every church group has its problems, including some impostors among the flock, perhaps even in positions of leadership.

Just as he keeps working with us individuals to help us grow up in the faith, Jesus works with churches to help them mature and do better. In the meantime, even a truly Christian church may have serious problems. For example, Jesus used the Apostle Paul to work with the church in Corinth, which at one point was having such serious problems that Paul told them,

"your meetings do more harm than good." —1 Corinthians 11:17 NIV

Some false teachers preached "another Jesus" to the church at Corinth (1 Cor. 11:4)—not the real Jesus whom Paul preached. The Corinthian church also tolerated sexual immorality in its midst. Paul also worked with the church at Galatia, where false teachers had introduced "a different gospel" (Gal. 1:6) that perverted the gospel of Christ. Speaking from heaven through a vision, the risen Christ had the Apostle John condemn the church at Thyatira for tolerating a woman who promoted sexual immorality. (Rev. 2:20) In fact, of the seven churches addressed in the opening chapters of Revelation, only two churches were found to be following Jesus acceptably; the other five were sternly warned to "repent." But that call to repentance meant Jesus was still working with them. So, if five out of seven churches in the first century needed to repent before they could receive Jesus' approval, what about the churches today? And what about their teaching?

If you want to follow Jesus—and not be misled by church leaders who are preaching "another Jesus"—prayerfully read the Bible.

And keep in mind that Jesus is alive. Besides living in heaven at the right hand of the Father, Jesus also is alive on earth, living with, in and through Christian believers. He promised:

"'One who has my commandments, and keeps them, that person is one who loves me. One who loves me will be loved by my Father, and I will love him, and will reveal myself to him. . . .

"'If a man loves me, he will keep my word. My Father will love him, and we will come to him, and make our home with him.

"'. . . But the Counselor, the Holy Spirit, whom the Father will send in my name, he will teach you all things, and will remind you of all that I said to you.'" —John 14:21, 23, 26

And Jesus is present in the meetings of the congregations of Christian believers:

"'Where two or three are gathered together in my name, there I am in their midst.'" —Matthew 18:20

So, when we fellowship with others, our focus should be on Jesus and not on the shortcomings of our fellow worshipers. Remember that we have our own shortcomings too, and the worldwide church is the body of Christ. Just as the different parts of our own physical bodies have their strengths and weaknesses, so the different members of the church each contribute different talents, and help each other with their weaknesses.

"Just as a body, though one, has many parts, but all its many parts form one body, so it is with Christ. For we were all baptized by one Spirit so as to form one body—whether Jews or Gentiles, slave or free. . . . Even so the body is not made up of one part but of many. . . .

The eye cannot say to the hand, 'I don't need you!' And the head cannot say to the feet, 'I don't need you!' On the contrary, those parts of the body that seem to be weaker are indispensable. . . .

Now you are the body of Christ, and each one of you is a part of it. And God has placed in the church first of all apostles, second prophets, third teachers, then miracles, then gifts of healing, of helping, of guidance, and of different kinds of tongues."

—1 Corinthians 12:12-14, 21-22, 27-28 NIV

Fellow believers can be a source of instruction and encouragement. And, as you grow in the faith, you will be able to help others in turn, especially as you become aware of the gifts and talents God has given you.

But beware of letting any church interpret the Bible for you, especially if the interpretation turns out to teach something different from what an ordinary person would understand from reading the Bible alone. Instead, become so familiar with the Bible itself that you can use it to evaluate the teachings you hear at church. Some pastors may resent your doing this, but those who follow Jesus and love the written word of God will welcome your using the Bible to check up on them. The Apostle Paul was glad when his listeners

"received the message with great eagerness and examined the Scriptures every day to see if what Paul said was true."

—Acts 17:11 NIV

Your prayer life

When we first embrace the Gospel message, we do it by putting faith in Jesus Christ and repenting of our sins—telling God in prayer that we are sorry for our sins and that we are now committing ourselves to follow Jesus as our Lord and Savior, recognizing in our prayer that Jesus died for our sins and rose again from the dead to give us everlasting life. But that sinner's prayer is only the beginning of a Christian's prayer life. Prayer should soon become a regular activity, as we grow in faith, trust and obedience.

Long before there was such a thing as a Jewish synagogue or a Christian church, there were faithful men who walked with God in a close personal relationship. They trusted, they obeyed and they prayed. They lived long before God revealed himself more fully through Jesus, but we can still learn about prayer from their examples.

Enoch was a great-grandson of a great-grandson of Adam.

"Enoch walked with God."   —Genesis 5:22, 24

Noah was the one God called to build an Ark for his family and the land animals to ride out the flood that would be sent to destroy a wicked world.

"Noah walked with God."   —Genesis 6:9

God is called in the Old Testament the "Hearer of prayer.":

"Hearer of prayer, to Thee all flesh cometh."

—Psalm 65:2 Young's Literal Translation

Yes, "all flesh"—everyone—is invited to come to God in prayer. The Apostle Paul told a pagan Greek audience that God is not far off from each one of us:

"He made from one blood every nation of men to dwell on all the surface of the earth, having determined appointed seasons, and the boundaries of their dwellings, that they should seek the Lord, if perhaps they might reach out for him and find him, though he is not far from each one of us."   —Acts 17:26-27

So, God hears the prayers of all sorts of people. He is not far off from each one of us. We don't need to go to a special place to pray. Nor do we need to assume any special posture. The Bible tells us that believers in the true God prayed in all sorts of positions and under all sorts of circumstances. King Solomon was leading a public assembly when

"Solomon prayed this prayer to the LORD, kneeling in front of the altar with his arms raised toward heaven."   —1 Kings 8:54 NCV

The elderly servant of the prophet Abraham was standing by a well when he had his camels kneel down to drink, but the Bible doesn't tell us what position the servant was in when he then prayed to God, and God answered his prayer. (Gen. 24:11-15)

Hannah, a woman in a troubled polygamous marriage, prayed silently to God while weeping bitterly in a public place, moving her lips but not making any sound:

"In bitterness of soul Hannah wept much and prayed to the LORD. . . . Hannah was praying in her heart, and her lips were moving but her voice was not heard. Eli thought she was drunk and said to her, 'How long will you keep on getting drunk? Get rid of your wine.' 'Not so, my lord,' Hannah replied, 'I am a woman who is deeply troubled. I have not been drinking wine or beer; I was pouring out my soul to the LORD.'" —1 Samuel 1:10-15 NIV

Nehemiah was one of the Jews living in foreign captivity, working as cup bearer for the king of the Medo-Persian empire, when he cried and fasted and prayed to God over several days before asking the king for permission to return and rebuild Jerusalem. Finally, while he was on the job as cup bearer, when the king noticed his distress and asked him how he could help, Nehemiah quickly prayed a silent prayer before answering. (Neh. 1:4-11; 2:4)

The Bible is full of many other examples demonstrating that you can pray to God in all sorts of circumstances, publicly or privately, silently or aloud. And the Bible also offers examples of what men and women of faith said in their prayers. Many of the psalms in the Bible book of Psalms are actually prayers to God. Consider for example this passage from Psalm 40:

"LORD, do not hold back your mercy from me; let your love and truth always protect me. Troubles have surrounded me; there are too many to count. My sins have caught me so that I cannot see a way to escape. I have more sins than hairs on my head, and I have lost my courage. Please, LORD, save me. Hurry, LORD, to help me." —Psalm 40:11-13 NCV

Jesus included in his teaching some instructions on how to pray—and how not to pray. He said that we should not pray for show, to impress other people who may be looking on or listening:

"'When you pray, you shall not be as the hypocrites, for they love to stand and pray in the synagogues and in the corners of the streets, that they may be seen by men. Most certainly, I tell you, they have received their reward.'" —Matthew 6:5

Showy prayers like that have their reward only in the admiration of other people, but have no reward from God. Rather, Jesus taught that most of our prayer life should be a private thing between ourselves and God:

"'But you, when you pray, enter into your inner room, and having shut your door, pray to your Father who is in secret, and your Father who sees in secret will reward you openly.'" —Matthew 6:6

Pagan idol worshipers commonly repeated repetitious prayers to their false gods. Jesus taught that we should not do that. The true God already knows our thoughts and our needs, even before we open our mouths:

"'In praying, don't use vain repetitions, as the Gentiles do; for they think that they will be heard for their much speaking. Therefore don't be like them, for your Father knows what things you need, before you ask him.'" —Matthew 6:7-8

When Jesus finished praying in a certain place, one of his followers asked him to teach them how to pray. In response, Jesus gave this model prayer as an example:

"He said to them, 'When you pray, say, "Our Father in heaven, may your name be kept holy. May your Kingdom come. May your will be done on earth, as it is in heaven. Give us day by day our daily bread. Forgive us our sins, for we ourselves also forgive everyone who is indebted to us. Bring us not into temptation, but deliver us from the evil one."'" —Luke 11:2-4

Moreover, shortly before he was arrested, Jesus told his disciples to pray to the Father in Jesus' name:

"'You didn't choose me, but I chose you, and appointed you, that you should go and bear fruit, and that your fruit should remain; that whatever you will ask of the Father in my name, he may give it to you.' . . .

"'In that day you will ask me no questions. Most certainly I tell you, whatever you may ask of the Father in my name, he will give it to you. Until now, you have asked nothing in my name. Ask, and you will receive, that your joy may be made full. I have spoken these things to you in figures of speech. But the time is coming when I will no more speak to you in figures of speech, but will tell you plainly about the Father. In that day you will ask in my name; and I don't say to you, that I will pray to the Father for you, for the Father himself loves you, because you have loved me, and have believed that I came forth from God.'" —John 15:16; 16:23-27

We can also learn from Jesus' own prayers that he prayed to his Father in heaven, as recorded in the Gospels. Sometimes Jesus went off to be alone in prayer:

"he went up into the mountain by himself to pray" —Matthew 14:23

Other times he spoke a brief prayer out loud in the midst of a crowd of people:

"At that time Jesus said, 'I praise you, Father, Lord of heaven and earth, because you have hidden these things from the wise and learned, and revealed them to little children. Yes, Father, for this was your good pleasure.'" —Matthew 11:25-26 NIV

The longest prayer of Christ recorded in the Scriptures is found in John chapter 17 where he prays for his disciples and for those who would become his followers in the future.

In the garden of Gethsemane, immediately before his arrest, the Gospels tell us Jesus prayed with great emotion:

"He went forward a little, fell on his face, and prayed, saying, 'My Father, if it is possible, let this cup pass away from me; nevertheless, not what I desire, but what you desire.' . . . Again, a second time he went away, and prayed, saying, 'My Father, if this cup can't pass away from me unless I drink it, your desire be done.'" —Matthew 26:39. 42

If we are struggling with unanswered prayer, the above passage can help us. Jesus wished the "cup" he was facing to pass away, but yielded his will to his heavenly Father's will. He prayed for the cup to pass away, but he ended up drinking it, because that was the Father's will.

The Apostle Paul also experienced unanswered prayer. He wrote,

"that I should not be exalted excessively, there was given to me a thorn in the flesh, a messenger of Satan to torment me, that I should not be exalted excessively. Concerning this thing, I begged the Lord three times that it might depart from me. He has said to me, 'My grace is sufficient for you, for my power is made perfect in weakness.' Most gladly therefore I will rather glory in my weaknesses, that the power of Christ may rest on me."

—2 Corinthians 12:7-9

So, the answer to Paul's prayer was No. But the Lord helped him to understand why it had to be that way. Like children with limited understanding, we may pray for things that we think best, but our heavenly Father sees aspects of our situation that we don't see and he knows what is really best in the long run.

We can also learn something else from the above passage: Paul was praying to Jesus. He wrote, "I begged the Lord," who answered him concerning "my power," and then Paul expressed contentment that "the power of Christ" rested on him. So the Lord who said "my power" was Christ.

Just as Paul spoke to Christ in prayer, we can do the same. Besides addressing prayer to "our Father," we can also speak to Jesus. Paul wrote that believers

"call on the name of our Lord Jesus Christ in every place."

—1 Corinthians 1:2

When the disciple Stephen was being stoned to death for his Christian witness, he called out in prayer to Jesus:

"They stoned Stephen as he called out, saying, 'Lord Jesus, receive my spirit!' He kneeled down, and cried with a loud voice, 'Lord, don't hold this sin against them!' When he had said this, he fell asleep." —Acts 7:59-60

Do you feel inadequate to come up with the right things to say in prayer? Don't worry about it. Even when you don't know how to pray as you should, the Holy Spirit will help you out:

"the Spirit helps us in our weakness. We do not know what we ought to pray for, but the Spirit himself intercedes for us with groans that words cannot express." —Romans 8:26 NIV

So, the burden is not on us to come up with the right words, or the right formula, in our prayers. God cares about us and knows what we need even before we ask. Jesus said,

"your Father knows what things you need, before you ask him."

—Matthew 6:8

And he added,

"'Ask, and it will be given you. Seek, and you will find. Knock, and it will be opened for you. For everyone who asks receives. He who seeks finds. To him who knocks it will be opened. Or who is there among you, who, if his son asks him for bread, will give him a stone? Or if he asks for a fish, who will give him a serpent? If you then, being evil, know how to give good gifts to your children, how much more will your Father who is in heaven give good things to those who ask him! '" —Matthew 7:7-11

Luke's account emphasizes that we need to persist in prayer, and to keep on asking:

"'I tell you, keep asking, and it will be given you. Keep seeking, and you will find. Keep knocking, and it will be opened to you.'"

—Luke 11:9

Luke also tells us that

"One day Jesus told his disciples a story to show that they should always pray and never give up." —Luke 18:1 New Living Translation

You may benefit from reading that story or parable for yourself in the eighteenth chapter of Luke's Gospel.

Our relationship with God as followers of his Son involves our heartfelt trust, our faithful obedience, our active service, and our fervent prayer. We listen to God as we prayerfully read his written Word. And we pray as we face life's challenges and as we go about our daily activities. Many Christians start each day with a time of prayer, or end each day that way. But we can also fill our day with prayer, silently giving thanks and asking for guidance as the need may be, throughout the day. The Apostle Paul urges us to

"pray continually" —1 Thessalonians 5:17

Know your Bible

If you wish to follow Jesus, the best way to learn how to do it is to prayerfully read the Bible. In his first letter to a young Christian leader named Timothy (a letter that became part of the Bible's New Testament) the Apostle Paul encouraged him to

"devote yourself to the public reading of Scripture"

—1 Timothy 4:13 NIV

And Paul's second letter to Timothy added this explanation:

"All Scripture is inspired by God and is useful to teach us what is true and to make us realize what is wrong in our lives. It straightens us out and teaches us to do what is right. It is God's way of preparing us in every way, fully equipped for every good thing God wants us to do." —2 Timothy 3:16-17 NLT

Reading the Bible may seem like an overwhelming task. After all, it is a big thick book filled with strange-sounding names and places. But it is well worth the effort. Reading while taking my daily walk on a treadmill, it takes me a little longer than a year to read the whole Bible, cover to cover. Having done this for years, I can no longer count how many times I've read it. Each time, I notice things I had not noticed before, learn new things and grow stronger in faith.

Each time I read through the Bible from cover to cover, I use a different translation. You may want to start out with a translation like the New Century Version (NCV) that renders the original Hebrew and Greek into simple English that is easy to understand.

Can an ordinary person really read the Bible and understand it? Well, there are plenty of preachers who will tell you No—either directly or subtly telling you that you need professional help to understand the Bible. They will gladly encourage you to listen to them instead of reading the Bible on your own. In fact, there were times in European history when church leaders and clergymen actively prevented people from reading Scripture, and even made doing so punishable by death. Lovers of the Bible like William Tyndale and John Huss were burned at the stake in the early 1500's for translating the Scriptures into their local language so that ordinary people could read the Bible. Corrupt church leaders at that time, eager to hold on to power and money, jealously guarded their position as the official interpreters of God's written Word.

Actually, one of the biggest lies told about the Bible is the claim that theologians and professional clergy are needed to explain and interpret it to the common man. That is a lie, because the Bible was written for the average man and woman to understand. It was written for dock workers and farm hands, housewives and laborers—not for intellectual professionals. As an author, I know it is easy to write a book that only educated intellectuals will understand; an author can accomplish this by using extremely complex sentence structure and technical jargon that the average person is unfamiliar with. But how can someone write a book that ordinary people can understand, while hiding its truths from well-educated intellectuals? That would be impossible for a human author. But God knows how to do this. In fact, that is what Jesus said to his heavenly Father in prayer concerning the Gospel message:

"Jesus said, 'I praise you, Father, Lord of heaven and earth, because you have hidden these things from the wise and learned, and revealed them to little children. Yes, Father, for this is what you were pleased to do.'" —Matthew 11:25-26 NIV

Simple, uneducated people can grasp the Gospel message when prayerfully reading the Bible, while highly-educated professionals often miss the point despite their scholarly study.

The Apostle Paul expressed a similar thought when he wrote this about the sort of people who grasp and respond to the message about Christ:

"It is written in the Scriptures: 'I will cause the wise to lose their wisdom; I will make the wise unable to understand.' [Isaiah 29:14] Where is the wise person? Where is the educated person? Where is the skilled talker of this world? . . . Brothers and sisters, look at what you were when God called you. Not many of you were wise in the way the world judges wisdom. . . . God chose the foolish things of the world to shame the wise . . ." —1 Corinthians 1:19-27 NCV

So, don't ever feel that you are unqualified to read the Bible on your own. Pray for understanding, and God will open up the meaning of the Scriptures to you as you read.

If you are reading the Bible for the first time, you may find it helpful to begin with the New Testament, starting in the Gospel of Matthew—so that you will be introduced right away to Jesus and his teachings. Then afterwards follow up by reading the Old Testament which provides the background that will give you a deeper understanding of the Christian message.

The first part of the Bible, the Old Testament, records the history of God's dealings with mankind from the creation of the first humans until around 2500 years ago. It explains how the first humans became separated from God through their own disobedience—and how their offspring spread out over the surface of the earth, multiplied rapidly and developed societies, cultures and religions devoid of any knowledge of the true God.

Eventually, God re-introduced himself to twelve tribes of slaves in Egypt, led them out of captivity, and established them as the nation of Israel, governed by laws God dictated to the prophet Moses. The first five books of the Bible—

Genesis, Exodus, Leviticus, Numbers and Deuteronomy—contain those laws. And the rest of the Old Testament tells how the people of Israel broke those laws over the following centuries. Meanwhile, the rest of the human race stumbled in darkness, guided by man-made philosophies and religions that barely reflected any recollection of the Creator their ancestors had abandoned thousands of years earlier.

The Old Testament also predicts a time when God would send his Messiah or Christ (meaning appointed leader) to bring people back to God—not just the Jews but people of all nations. At God's appointed time, he stepped in by sending his Son to earth—born as a human child to a carpenter's virgin wife in the town of Bethlehem, not far from Jerusalem.

The Bible's New Testament begins with four accounts of Jesus' life and teachings. These Gospels of Matthew, Mark, Luke and John all tell how Jesus called the Jewish people back to God and assigned his followers the work of taking his message to all races and nations around the world. They also tell how Jesus gave his life sacrificially—through a horribly painful death on a Roman execution cross—to ransom the rest of us from sin and death. Yes, he died in our place, so that we might have the hope of eternal life. More than that, he rose from the dead on the third day, was seen by hundreds of eye witnesses, and now lives at the right hand of God the Father in heaven. He is the living Savior of all who turn to him in faith and obedience.

The Acts of the Apostles follows the four Gospels in our Bibles. Written by a medical doctor named Luke, a traveling companion of the Apostle Paul, who also wrote the Gospel of Luke, the book of Acts details the spread of Christianity into Europe and Asia Minor.

The rest of the New Testament consists mainly of letters written by Paul, the Apostles Peter and John, and early disciples James and Jude. These letters address issues that troubled the early churches, and they provide guidance for everyone who wants to follow Jesus.

Our Bibles conclude with the book of Revelation, a prophetic vision the risen Christ gave to the Apostle John while John was in prison for preaching the Gospel.

A collection of sixty-six books and letters by dozens of different writers, the Bible was written over a span of roughly 1600 years. The books and letters are arranged partly according to chronology, but are also grouped together according to whether they are histories, letters, prophetic writings or poetic, so they are not found in a strictly chronological order.

Here is a more detailed introduction to the various books of the Bible:

OLD TESTAMENT

Genesis

The first of the five Books of Moses, Genesis tells the history of mankind from the very beginning. It recounts how God created the first human pair and how they rebelled against God's commands and thus brought sin into the world and passed on a sinful nature—an inborn tendency to sin—to their offspring. The world of Adam and Eve's offspring eventually became so corrupt that God sent a flood to wipe mankind off the face of the earth, except for four married couples who were preserved in a huge floating box or ark.

Genesis then goes on to record how the planet was repopulated from these four couples. After several generations their descendents forgot about God and became technologically advanced enough to build a city and begin working on a skyscraper, but God intervened by causing different family groups to speak different languages, so they could not understand each other any longer and had to abandon the project. Those family groups then separated and spread abroad on the earth. Genesis details how their offspring became the ancestors of the races and nations we know today.

Mankind in general took up worshiping idols made of wood, stone or metal, but a few individuals remained faithful to the true God, the Creator. The Genesis account tells the history of one of these individuals, Abraham, who became the ancestor of the nations that eventually inhabited the areas now covered by Israel, Jordan, Syria and Lebanon. God made a covenant (formal agreement) with Abraham to make him a father of nations and to give the land of Canaan to his offspring. Abraham questioned God about his plan to destroy the wicked men of Sodom and Gomorrah—an episode that is referred back to in other books of the Bible as a warning example.

Abraham's grandson Jacob was renamed Israel, and became the father of the Jewish people. So, Genesis then begins the story of the Jews, who were selected by the Creator to preserve this early history, to receive and preserve God's written laws by writing the Bible, and to suffer many things over the centuries as instructive examples for the rest of mankind..

Exodus

Although they had immigrated to Egypt originally as honored guests, Israel's descendents were later forced into slavery to the Egyptians. Exodus records how God intervened to remind a new generation who he is, and to free that generation of Israelites from slavery and lead them out of Egypt.

It tells the life story of Moses, who is credited with writing the first five books of the Bible. These five books—Genesis, Exodus, Leviticus, Numbers and Deuteronomy—set out more than six hundred laws given by God to the Jewish people. These laws were part of a formal agreement or covenant between God and the people of Israel.

As you read the laws promulgated in the books of Moses, keep in mind that they fall into different groups.

Some were laws designed to keep the Jewish people separate and apart from their neighbors, so that they could preserve intact their identity as a separate people to serve a unique purpose down through the centuries, and not eventually blend in with the rest of mankind. (Regulations requiring the Jews to eat special food, and to dress and groom in peculiar ways, were among the laws given to keep them separate from their neighbors.)

Others were ceremonial laws detailing how God wanted the Israelites to worship him—through rituals and animal sacrifices that symbolically foreshadowed the sacrificial death of the Messiah to come. These laws regarding worship also taught general principles that apply to all mankind in our relationship with God.

And other laws taught the Jews how God wanted them to behave in all aspects of their lives. These laws, too, shed light on how God wants all of us to behave. For example, some regulated business dealings: "Don't cheat hired servants who are poor and needy, whether they are fellow Israelites or foreigners living in one of your towns." (Deut. 24:14 NCV) Other regulations required kindness to animals: "When an ox is working in the grain, do not cover its mouth to keep it from eating." (Deut. 25:4 NCV) Others set standards for sanitation: "When you are camped in time of war . . . Choose a place outside the camp where people may go to relieve themselves. Carry a tent peg with you, and when you relieve yourself, dig a hole and cover up your dung." (Deut. 23:9-13 NCV) Many laws required the Jews to treat people fairly and kindly: "If an escaped slave comes to you, do not hand over the slave to his master. Let the slave live with you anywhere he likes, in any town he chooses. Do not mistreat him." (Deut. 23:15-16 NCV) Although these laws strictly applied only to those under their jurisdiction—the Jewish people—they give us insight into how God wants people to treat one another in matters involving property, business dealings, marriage, sexual morality, and daily life..

Leviticus

This Bible book takes its name from Levi, one of Israel's twelve sons whose offspring were selected to serve as priests, temple workers and teachers of God's law to the nation descended from Israel. Leviticus continues to spell out these laws in detail. It also begins to enumerate the punishments God would bring on the Jewish nation if they failed to keep God's laws. Eventually, if they persisted in breaking his laws and refused to repent, God said, "I will scatter you among the nations and will draw out my sword and pursue you. Your land will be laid waste, and your cities will lie in ruins."—Lev. 26:33 NIV

Numbers

This book of Moses takes its name from the fact that it begins with a census numbering "all the men in Israel twenty years old or more who are able to serve in the army." (Num. 1:3 NIV) It details the wanderings of the twelve tribes of Israel through wilderness and desert lands, and records events that give insight into God's ways of dealing with mankind.

Deuteronomy

The last of the five books of Moses, Deuteronomy summarizes and repeats some of the material of the other four, restating the Ten Commandments and various laws as well as retelling some of the history of the Israelites from shortly after their departure from Egypt until the death of Moses across the Jordan River from the Promised Land.

A number of chapters in Deuteronomy are devoted to outlining the blessings that would come to the Jewish people if they kept God's laws and the curses that would come upon them if they broke God's laws. Ultimately, if they failed to keep their agreement with God, he would drive them out of the Promised Land. Moreover, he told them, "You will become a thing of horror and an object of scorn and ridicule to all the nations where the LORD will drive you. . . . the LORD will scatter you among all nations, from one end of the earth to the other." (Deut. 28:37, 64 NIV) This prophecy was fulfilled hundreds of years later, and its fulfillment continued even thousands of years later, into modern times. The worldwide "scorn and ridicule" against the Jews came to be called "anti-Semitism," and the Jewish people were scattered among all the nations until the rebirth of the nation of Israel in 1948.

Moses completed the writing of the first five books of the Bible before his death some time around 1500 years before the birth of Christ, and the books of Moses are referred to and quoted from in many of the later books of the Bible.

Joshua

Moses died at the edge of the Promised Land, leaving the people under the command of Joshua who had been his lieutenant. The book of Joshua documents the Israelites' miraculous crossing of the Jordan River into the land of Canaan, and their conquest of the land, eventually dividing it among their tribes.

Judges

Instructed by God to annihilate the wicked inhabitants of Canaan, the Israelites failed to do so completely. As a result they were repeatedly ensnared by the false gods and idols worshipped by those people, and God punished them by allowing nearby enemies to harass and dominate them. Then God would raise up a "judge" or liberator to defeat the oppressors. This book takes its name from those judges.

Far from being saintly, perfect figures, the Bible reveals the humanity, frailty and sinfulness even of such heroic personages—this candid honesty serving as evidence of the divine inspiration of the Scriptures in an age when leaders of pagan nations were usually painted in glowing terms.

Ruth

During a time of famine a couple from Bethlehem took refuge in the nearby land of Moab, together with their two sons. The husband died, and the two sons married Moabite women. Then the sons died as well, leaving the Israelite woman and her two daughters-in-law, one of whom was named Ruth. Since the famine was over, the Israelite woman decided to return home. When she said goodbye to her daughters-in-law, Ruth insisted on going home with her instead of returning to her own people. "Where you go I will go, and where you stay I will stay," she said. "Your people will be my people and your God my God." (Ruth 1:16 NIV)

More than just a sweet story of loyalty, the book of Ruth concludes by telling how this Moabite woman took her place in the family line that later gave birth to king David. And since Jesus' mother Mary and foster father Joseph were both descendents of David, Ruth's story also provides details of the ancestry of the Messiah.

1 & 2 Samuel

Likely written between 1000 B.C. and 1100 B.C., or thereabouts, the books of First and Second Samuel tell how God called a young boy, Samuel, to serve as his prophet, and how the nation of Israel came to be ruled by a king—first Saul from the tribe of Benjamin and then David from the tribe of Judah.

David was a mere shepherd boy, the youngest among several brothers, but demonstrated courage and trust in God when he battled the Philistine warrior Goliath one-on-one, and God chose David to replace unfaithful Saul. Yet even David is presented in these books with all his flaws and weaknesses, in contrast to the way histories of pagan nations of that time portrayed their kings as godlike heroes—again showing how the books of the Bible inspired by God differ from mere writings of men.

Besides continuing to establish the royal lineage of the coming Messiah, these books also offer insight into God's dealings with those who are chosen to serve him, both those who serve faithfully and those who deviate from God's instructions.

1 & 2 Kings

These books cover hundreds of years of history, from the final days of king David to the fall of Jerusalem to the Babylonian Empire—or from roughly 1000 B.C. to around 600 B.C.

God instructed David to have his son build a temple in Jerusalem. King Solomon carried that out and was blessed with a peaceful reign lasting many decades. Solomon was faithful to God during the early years of his reign, but married many foreign women who eventually led him to share in worshiping false gods and idols.

Soon after Solomon's death most of the tribes of Israel rejected his son and chose their own king. The nation split into the northern kingdom of Israel and the southern kingdom of Judah. Israel set up golden idols to be worshipped in two northern cities, so that subjects would not have to go to Jerusalem to worship at the temple in the southern kingdom's territory. Even the successive kings of Judah varied in their faithfulness to God, many of them promoting idolatry instead.

Eventually the Jerusalem temple fell into disuse and disrepair, and the books of Moses containing God's covenant and laws were lost and forgotten. Finally during the reign of king Josiah the books of Moses were found in the temple. The king read them aloud to the people, including the warnings mentioned above in Leviticus and Deuteronomy that the nation would be destroyed and its people scattered abroad if they proved unfaithful. 2 Kings records the fulfillment of this prophecy when God sent the Babylonian Empire to destroy Jerusalem.

1 & 2 Chronicles

While the history in 1 & 2 Kings alternates back and forth between discussing events in the northern kingdom of Israel and the southern kingdom of Judah, the account in 1 & 2 Chronicles covers roughly the same time span from the standpoint of Judah alone, for the most part. It begins with extensive genealogical records, tracing the descent of mankind from Noah, and then focusing on the genealogy of the twelve tribes of Israel. 2 Chronicles concludes with a summary of the Jews' decades-long captivity in Babylon, followed by the decree of Persian king Cyrus for the Jewish people to return to Jerusalem and rebuild the temple.

Ezra

The Babylonian Empire that destroyed Jerusalem and carried the Jews captive to Babylon was eventually itself defeated by the empire of the Medes and Persians. Ezra begins with the official proclamation of king Cyrus of Persia for the Jews to return to Jerusalem and rebuild the temple. It details the numbers who returned and the names of prominent individuals among them. Ezra himself was one of the priests who returned His book also relates the conflicts that occurred with non-Jews who had been transplanted into the land by conquering empires, and the conflicts among the Jews themselves as their leaders sought to re-establish temple worship and the laws given through Moses.

Nehemiah

A descendent of Jews who had been taken captive decades earlier, Nehemiah was cupbearer to Artaxerxes, ruler of the Medo-Persian empire, when it came to his attention that the work of rebuilding Jerusalem had stopped. Nehemiah used his influence to obtain a letter from king Artaxerxes authorizing him to restart that work. Nehemiah mentions Ezra the priest, and his book overlaps with Ezra's account, but also continues through to the completion of rebuilding Jerusalem's wall.

Esther

The book of Esther details an attempt by Haman, the Persian king's prime minister, to exterminate the Jews throughout the Medo-Persian empire which, at that time, ruled most of the lands where Jews had been scattered during their captivity. It relates how a young Jewish woman named Esther worked with her uncle Mordecai to foil the plot. Through God's providence, Esther became queen of the empire, Mordecai became prime minister, and the plot to kill all the Jews was turned into a triumph for them instead—an episode still commemorated today in the Jewish festival of Purim.

(Modern readers of Ezra, Nehemiah and Esther may draw parallels with the time when a Jew became prime minister of the British Empire, the occasion when a different British prime minister issued an official letter promising a national home for the Jewish people in Palestine, and the time when a European ruler again attempted to annihilate the Jewish people through the Holocaust.)

Job

The book of Job tells the story of a good and faithful individual named Job who was blessed by God, but whose faith was tested by sudden loss and adversity. The veil is pulled back to show us the assembly of angels in the presence of God. Satan enters the assembly and accuses Job of living right only for selfish reasons, to receive God's material blessings. To prove Satan wrong, God allows him to take those blessings away, but Job still maintains his faithfulness. So, Satan demands the opportunity to afflict Job with sickness, which God again allows. Job suffers greatly, but remains faithful through it all.

Much of the book is filled with the sayings of four friends of Job who come to comfort him, but who speak falsehood, accusing him of sin. In their view, Job's sufferings must be due to sin on his part. Their false teachings are similar to the false 'health and wealth gospel' that is popular in some churches today—the false teaching that Christianity is a sure path to physical health and financial prosperity, and that sickness reflects sin in a Christian's life.

Although the authorship of the book of Job is uncertain, we know that it is quite ancient, because the prophet Ezekiel who was among the Jewish exiles in Babylon mentions Job by name (Ezek. 14:14, 20), as does the New Testament writer James. (James 5:11)

Psalms

The book of Psalms is a collection of inspired songs and poetic prayers composed by a number of early writers, including king David, over a period of roughly five hundred years, from around 1000 B.C. to around 500 B.C. Psalm

117 is the shortest, just two verses, and Psalm 119 is the longest at 176 verses. (The chapter and verse numbers were added in more recent times, as is the case with all of the books in the Bible.)

More than just poetry and songs of praise, the Psalms also contain inspired prophecies that were fulfilled centuries later. For example, Psalm 22 begins with the words Jesus spoke on the cross, "My God, my God, why have you forsaken me?" (Ps. 22:1; Matt. 27:46 NIV) and goes on to say, "they have pierced my hands and my feet." (Ps.22:16 NIV)

Proverbs

The book of Proverbs is a collection of wise sayings, most of them attributed to king Solomon. "The fear of the LORD is the beginning of knowledge," according to Proverbs 1:7 (KJV).

Ecclesiastes

Unusual in its style, the book of Ecclesiastes presents a debate between a speaker who sees life as meaningless and vain, and another speaker who sees life as meaningful due to our relationship with God—although the two speakers may represent an internal debate within the mind of the writer. In the end it is the viewpoint shaped by knowledge of God that wins:

"This is the end of the matter. All has been heard. Fear God, and keep his commandments; for this is the whole duty of man. For God will bring every work into judgment, with every hidden thing, whether it is good, or whether it is evil." (Eccl. 12:13-14)

Song of Songs

Also referred to as "Song of Solomon" this book of the Bible is a poetic story of love. The main speakers are a young shepherd girl and the young man she loves. Many readers see this as an allegorical representation of the relationship between God and the nation of Israel, or between Christ and the Church as portrayed much later in the book of Revelation:

"'. . . the marriage of the Lamb has come, and his wife has made herself ready.' It was given to her that she would array herself in bright, pure, fine linen: for the fine linen is the righteous acts of the saints. . . . I saw the holy city, New Jerusalem, coming down out of heaven from God, prepared like a bride adorned for her husband. . . . One of the seven angels . . . spoke with me, saying, 'Come here. I will show you the wife, the Lamb's bride.' . . . and showed me the holy city, Jerusalem, coming down out of heaven from God . . ." (Rev. 19:7-8; 21:2, 9-10)

Isaiah

The prophet Isaiah served God during the reigns of Uzziah, Jotham, Ahaz and Hezekiah, kings of Judah. His book contains prophecies as well as history that overlaps the history found in some of the later chapters of 2 Kings and 2

Chronicles. Isaiah boldly proclaimed the coming judgment of God against the unfaithful Jewish nation, telling them, "Hear the word of the LORD, you rulers of Sodom; listen to the law of our God, you people of Gomorrah!" (Isa. 1:10 NIV) Concerning Jerusalem, he said, "See how the faithful city has become a harlot!" (Isa. 1:21 NIV)

Isaiah also prophesied concerning other nations in the Middle East and North Africa. And he spoke of events in the distant future concerning the coming Messiah or Christ:

"For to us a child is born, to us a son is given, and the government will be on his shoulders. And he will be called Wonderful Counselor, Mighty God, Everlasting Father, Prince of Peace. Of the increase of his government and peace there will be no end. He will reign on David's throne and over his kingdom, establishing and upholding it with justice and righteousness from that time on and forever." (Isa. 9:6-7 NIV)

"But he was pierced for our transgressions, he was crushed for our iniquities; the punishment that brought us peace was upon him, and by his wounds we are healed." (Isa. 53:5 NIV)

Jesus read publicly from the book of Isaiah when he visited the synagogue in Nazareth, the town where he had grown up, and stated, "Today, this Scripture has been fulfilled in your hearing." (Luke 4:16-21; Isa. 61:1-2)

Jeremiah

Jeremiah, a priest at the temple in Jerusalem around 600 B.C., served as God's prophet during the final years of the kingdom of Judah. He saw the destruction of Jerusalem, with the Jewish king and leading men carried off captive to Babylon. There were many other prophets in Jerusalem at that time, but they spoke lies in God's name, denying the coming judgment that Jeremiah boldly proclaimed.

Besides foretelling events that occurred later during his own lifetime, Jeremiah also recorded God's promise of the new covenant or agreement that we read about in the New Testament:

"'The time is coming,' declares the LORD, 'when I will make a new covenant with the house of Israel and with the house of Judah. It will not be like the covenant I made with their forefathers when I took them by the hand to lead them out of Egypt, because they broke my covenant, though I was a husband to them,' declares the LORD. 'This is the covenant I will make with the house of Israel after that time,' declares the LORD. 'I will put my laws in their minds and write it on their hearts. I will be their God, and they will be my people. No longer will a man teach his neighbor, or a man his brother, saying, "Know the LORD," because they will all know me, from the least of them to the greatest,' declares the LORD. 'For I will forgive their wickedness and will remember their sins no more.'" (Jer. 31:31-34 NIV)

Lamentations

Attributed to the prophet Jeremiah, the book of Lamentations is a series of mournful poems expressing grief over the destruction of Jerusalem:

"How deserted lies the city, once so full of people!" (Lam. 1:1 NIV) "The punishment of my people is greater than that of Sodom," the poet laments. "....it happened because of the sins of her prophets and the iniquities of her priests . . . The LORD himself has scattered them." (Lam. 4:6, 13, 16 NIV)

Ezekiel

The prophet Ezekiel was among prominent Jews taken into exile by Babylon a few years before the rest of the Jews were taken away and Jerusalem was destroyed. He wrote while he was "among the exiles by the Kebar River." (Ezek. 1:1 NIV)

God showed Ezekiel visions of heavenly things, and had him proclaim judgments against the Jews and against the surrounding nations. Toward the end of his book, the prophecies move ahead to the distant future to a time when the Jews would be once again "gathered from many nations to the mountains of Israel" (Ezek. 38:8 NIV) and when their restored nation would be attacked by "Gog, of the land of Magog" along with armies from many other nations including "Persia" (now called Iran). (Ezek. 38:3-6 NIV) But God will "pour down torrents of rain, hailstones and burning sulfur on him and on his troops and on the many nations with him." (Ezek. 38:22-23 NIV)

Daniel

Daniel was just a teenager when the Jewish royal family and nobility were taken into exile, and God gave him such wisdom that he was selected to serve in the court of the king of Babylon. Some of his prophecies involved things that would happen to the Babylonian empire and its king, but most of the visions God gave him pointed toward events in the distant future.

Daniel prophesied in detail concerning a long succession of kingdoms and governments, after which "the God of heaven will set up a kingdom that will never be destroyed, nor will it be left to another people. It will crush all those kingdoms and bring them to an end, but it will itself endure forever." (Dan. 2:44 NIV) This would not be just another human government, but there would be "someone like a son of man" who would go into God's very presence in heaven to rule everlastingly and to be worshiped by "all peoples, nations and men of every language." (Dan. 7:13-14 NIV) When Jesus identified himself as "the Son of Man sitting at the right hand of Power, and coming on the clouds of the sky," the Jewish high court condemned him for blasphemy. (Matt. 26:64-65)

In the ninth chapter of Daniel a timetable is given for when the Messiah or Christ would come, and it points to the year when Jesus began his public ministry.

Hosea

The prophet Hosea served God during the final decades of the kingdoms of Israel and Judah. God commanded him to marry an unfaithful wife, a prostitute, to illustrate the unfaithfulness of Israel and Judah. And to illustrate how God repeatedly forgave his people, he commanded Hosea, "Go, show your love to your wife again, though she is loved by another and is an adulteress. Love her as the LORD loves the Israelites, though they turn to other gods." (Hos. 3:1 NIV) Hosea's prophecies speak of God's anger toward Israel, and the blessings that would come when the nation would repent.

Joel

The prophet Joel spoke to the people of Israel concerning a devastating invasion of locusts, which he compared to an army sent by God, and called them to repent in the face of God's judgment. The book also speaks of future blessings for Israel, and tells of the coming judgment against the Gentile nations.

"For, behold, in those days, and in that time, when I restore the fortunes of Judah and Jerusalem, I will gather all nations, and will bring them down into the valley of Jehoshaphat; and I will execute judgment on them there for my people, and for my heritage, Israel, whom they have scattered among the nations. They have divided my land, and have cast lots for my people . . ." (Joel 3:1-2)

Amos

Amos was not a prophet, but was a shepherd herding sheep and tending sycamore fig trees during the reigns of the second king Jereboam of Israel and king Uzziah of Judah. But then God called Amos to proclaim a message of judgment to the people of Israel and to the surrounding nations. (Amos 7:14-15)

Although the Jews were living in security at that time, Amos delivered God's message that he would destroy their nation and "sift the house of Israel among all the nations, as grain is sifted in a sieve." Yet later, God would "bring my people Israel back from captivity, and they will rebuild the ruined cities, and inhabit them." (Amos 9:9, 14)

Obadiah

The shortest book of the Hebrew scriptures, just twenty-one verses long, the book of Obadiah foretells disaster for the neighboring nation of Edom and a restoration of blessings to the Jewish people.

Jonah

Called by God to travel to the large foreign city Nineveh and there preach a judgment message, Jonah ran away instead. He boarded a ship to flee to the opposite end of the Mediterranean Sea, but when the sailors realized their ship was about to sink in a storm due to Jonah's presence on board, they threw him overboard. Swallowed alive by a huge fish, Jonah repented and prayed to God, after which he made it back to shore and took up the missionary assignment God had given him.

However, Jonah's rebellious personality continued to trouble him. When the people of Nineveh repented and God listened to their prayers by holding off the promised destruction of their city, Jonah responded with anger instead of appreciation.

The book of Jonah gives great insight into God's mercy toward people like the pagans of Nineveh "who can't discern between their right hand and their left hand" (Jonah 4:11), and also shows how he can use even stubborn and rebellious individuals like Jonah to preach his message.

Those who are inclined to dismiss the book of Jonah as a children's story should note that Jesus referred to it as factual. He said, "For as Jonah was three days and three nights in the belly of the whale, so will the Son of Man be three days and three nights in the heart of the earth. The men of Nineveh will stand up in the judgment with this generation, and will condemn it, for they repented at the preaching of Jonah; and behold, someone greater than Jonah is here." (Matt. 12:40-41; compare Luke 11:29-32)

Micah

The prophet Micah foretold the destruction coming on the ancient kingdoms of Israel and Judah. He also declared God's message that he would restore the Jews to their land in the distant future.

Micah also foretold that the Messiah or Christ would come from Bethlehem. (Compare Micah 5:2 and Matthew 2:1-6) And he wrote the familiar words that describe the peace that will prevail when Christ rules the earth:

"They will beat their swords into plowshares, and their spears into pruning hooks. Nation will not lift up sword against nation, neither will they learn war any more." (Micah 4:3)

Nahum

Although the city of Nineveh repented when Jonah preached there, and was spared destruction at that time, the prophet Nahum evidently spoke at a different time, and proclaimed God's judgment against that ancient city:

"Your people are scattered on the mountains, and there is no one to gather them. There is no healing your wound, for your injury is fatal. All who hear the report of you clap their hands over you; for who hasn't felt your endless cruelty?" (Nahum 3:18-19)

Habakkuk

The book of Habakkuk begins with a back and forth dialog between the prophet by that name and God concerning the sins of the Jewish nation and the destruction about to come at the hands of the Babylonian empire. Then it concludes with a prophetic prayer by the prophet.

Zephaniah

The prophecy of "Zephaniah, the son of Cushi, the son of Gedaliah, the son of Amariah, the son of Hezekiah, in the days of Josiah, the son of Amon, king of Judah" begins with a warning of the impending destruction of Judah and Jerusalem as punishment for their unfaithfulness to God. (Zeph. 1:1) Then it goes on to pronounce God's judgments against the surrounding nations, and the eventual restoration of Jerusalem.

Haggai

During the second year of Medo-Persian emperor Darius, the prophet Haggai proclaimed God's messages to the Jews who had returned from exile to rebuild Jerusalem and its temple. They had been back in the Promised Land for around seventeen or eighteen years, but had not yet completed the work of rebuilding the temple. Haggai's message spurred them on to finish that work.

Zechariah

A contemporary of Haggai, Zechariah also presented visions from God to spur on the rebuilding of the temple in Jerusalem after the Jews returned from exile in Babylon. He also prophesied concerning the future Messiah or Christ that he would come to Jerusalem "righteous, and having salvation; lowly, and riding on a donkey, even on a colt, the foal of a donkey" (Zech. 9:9; compare Matt. 21:5, John 12:15), that the price of his betrayal would be "thirty pieces of silver" (Zech. 11:13; compare Matt. 26:15, 27:9), that he would be pierced on the cross (Zech. 12:10; compare John 19:37), and that his disciples would then be scattered (Zech. 13:7; compare Matt. 26:31, Mark 14:27)

Zechariah also foretells a time when Jerusalem will become "a burdensome stone for all the peoples. . . . and all the nations of the earth will be gathered together against it." (Zech. 12:3)

Malachi

The last book of the Old Testament in our Bibles, Malachi appears to have been written after the Jews returned from exile in Babylon to live again in the Promised Land. Although merely four chapters long, it is quoted or paraphrased numerous times in the New Testament. Malachi points out the sins of the Israelites and their priests, and calls them to repent. Through the prophet, God tells them, "Then I will come to you and judge you. I will be quick to testify against those who take part in evil magic, adultery, and lying under oath, those who cheat workers of their pay and who cheat widows and orphans, those who are unfair to foreigners, and those who do not respect me." (Mal. 3:5 NCV)

NEW TESTAMENT

Matthew

According to early Church writers the Apostle Matthew wrote his account of Jesus' life and ministry first, before Mark, Luke and John, and wrote it in Hebrew, the language of the earliest disciples. The four Gospels each present the works and teachings of Jesus Christ from a slightly different perspective. (If you are interested in comparing them, side by side, you may wish to consult a book such as my *Parallel Gospels in Harmony—with Study Guide* or the free online version of that book at http://www.ParallelGospels.NET)

Matthew's Gospel begins with Jesus' royal genealogy through his foster-father Joseph, a descendent of king David. Matthew also relates the details of Jesus' birth from Joseph's perspective.

Matthew's account emphasizes the fulfillment of prophecies from the Hebrew Scriptures—prophecies that pointed to the promised Messiah, and that Jesus fulfilled.

Mark

The shortest of the four Gospels, Mark's is a fast-moving account, traditionally based on what he remembered hearing about Jesus' life and ministry at the Apostle Peter's feet. It omits some of Jesus' longer talks, such as the Sermon on the Mount and parables about the Kingdom recorded by Matthew and Luke, and Jesus' final words to his followers recorded by John.

But, for the most part, the Gospels of Matthew, Mark and Luke cover the same ground, each one occasionally supplying some details omitted by the others.

Luke

The physician Luke accompanied the Apostle Paul on his missionary travels among the Gentiles, and wrote his Gospel in Greek for a cosmopolitan Greek audience.

The account begins with the birth of John the baptizer who would later introduce Jesus to the Jewish people, and then goes on to relate the story of Jesus' birth from the perspective of his mother Mary, followed by Jesus' royal genealogy through Mary who was, like her husband Joseph, a descendant of king David.

Luke also wrote the book of Acts, which takes up where his Gospel account leaves off.

John

Church tradition tells us that the aged Apostle John wrote his account last, after the other three were already circulating among the churches. John's Gospel stresses a close, personal relationship with Jesus.

The other three are often referred to as the Synoptic Gospels because they refer to the same events and the same messages Jesus delivered, while John, although telling the same story, also supplies information on a number of events and messages not included in the other Gospels. For example, only John tells of the resurrection of Lazarus and Jesus' final sermon to his closest disciples before his arrest.

Acts

The medical doctor Luke wrote the Acts of the Apostles as a sequel to his Gospel account. He covers the growth and spread of the Christian congregation from the days immediately following Jesus' resurrection, through the missionary tours of the Apostle Paul around the eastern Mediterranean, to Paul's transport to Rome as a prisoner in chains. Luke shared in some of those travels with Paul, as can be seen from his use of the first person ("we") in some passages.

Romans

The Apostle Paul's letter to the church in Rome was written before he visited the city. He spoke of man's rebellion against God and explained that, "sin entered into the world through one man, and death through sin; and so death passed to all men, because all sinned." (Rom. 5:12) And he reviewed how far man had fallen: "Professing themselves to be wise, they became fools, and traded the glory of the incorruptible God for the likeness of an image of corruptible man, and of birds, and four-footed animals, and creeping things. Therefore God also gave them up in the lusts of their hearts to uncleanness, that their bodies should be dishonored among themselves, who exchanged the truth of God for a lie, and worshiped and served the creature rather than the Creator, who is blessed forever. Amen. For this reason, God gave them up to vile passions. For their women changed the natural function into that which is against nature. Likewise also the men, leaving the natural function of the woman, burned in their lust toward one another, men doing what is inappropriate with men, and receiving in themselves the due penalty of their error." (Rom. 1:22-27)

He also addressed issues the churches faced over how to deal with the laws of Moses, which some wanted to impose on the Gentile believers. These words from this letter encourage us when we feel that we are at a loss as to how to pray: "the Spirit also helps our weaknesses, for we don't know how to pray as we ought. But the Spirit himself makes intercession for us with groanings which can't be uttered." (Rom. 8:26)

1 and 2 Corinthians

Paul's letters to the church in Corinth cover many topics of concern to that congregation and helpful to followers of Jesus today. We also get some insight into the hardships of Paul's travels: "Five times from the Jews I received forty stripes minus one. Three times I was beaten with rods. Once I was stoned. Three times I suffered shipwreck. I have been a night and a day in the deep. I have been in travels often, perils of rivers, perils of robbers, perils from my countrymen, perils from the Gentiles, perils in the city, perils in the wilderness, perils in the sea, perils among false brothers." (2 Cor. 11:24-26)

In his first letter Paul addressed a case of blatant sexual immorality that was allowed to go on unchecked among the membership. He instructed the leaders of the church to expel the guilty individual. Later, in his second letter, he encouraged them to readmit this individual who had since accepted correction and repented.

Paul also encouraged all of us by writing this about the temptations we face in this world: "No temptation has taken you except what is common to man. God is faithful, who will not allow you to be tempted above what you are able, but will with the temptation also make the way of escape, that you may be able to endure it." (1 Cor. 10:13)

Have you been troubled by unanswered prayer? Paul suffered from a personal affliction, and prayed three times for it to go away, but the answer was No. He wrote, "there was given to me a thorn in the flesh, a messenger of Satan to torment me, that I should not be exalted excessively. Concerning this thing, I begged the Lord three times that it might depart from me. He has said to me, 'My grace is sufficient for you, for my power is made perfect in weakness.' Most gladly therefore I will rather glory in my weaknesses, that the power of Christ may rest on me." (2 Cor. 12:7-9) Besides helping us understand that the answer to our own prayers may sometimes be No, this passage also refutes the false 'health and wealth gospel' that is taught in some churches today—the false teaching that Christianity is a sure path to physical health and financial prosperity, and that believers fall sick only when there is sin in their lives.

Just as the church in Corinth was misled by false teachers, so likewise churches today may have pastors who fail to follow the real Jesus, the Jesus of the Bible. Paul chided the Corinthians, "But I am afraid that somehow, as the serpent deceived Eve in his craftiness, so your minds might be corrupted from the simplicity that is in Christ. For if he who comes preaches another Jesus, whom we did not preach, or if you receive a different spirit, which you did not receive, or a different 'good news,' which you did not accept, you put up with that well enough." (2 Cor. 11:3-4) We should not put up with pastors who preach a different Jesus. And the only way we can identify and avoid them is by reading the Bible for ourselves, so that we can spot counterfeit teachings, teachings that don't reflect the message we find in the Bible.

Galatians

The Apostle Paul's letter "to the churches in Galatia" (Gal. 1:2 NIV) indicates that false teachers were active there, too, and that believers were being deceived by them: "I am astonished that you are so quickly deserting the one who called you by the grace of Christ and are turning to a different gospel—which is really no gospel at all. Evidently some people are throwing you into confusion and are trying to pervert the gospel of Christ." (Gal. 1:6-7 NIV)

The letter to the Galatians makes it clear that Christians are not under the jurisdiction of the laws given to the Jewish nation through Moses. "The law was our guardian leading us to Christ so that we could be made right with God through faith. Now the way of faith has come, and we no longer live under a guardian." (Gal. 3:24-25 NCV) Instead, Paul tells Christians to "Live by following the Spirit." (Gal. 5:16)

Those led by God's Holy Spirit produce the fruits of the Spirit, not the works of the flesh: "Now the works of the flesh are obvious, which are: adultery, sexual immorality, uncleanness, lustfulness, idolatry, sorcery, hatred, strife, jealousies, outbursts of anger, rivalries, divisions, heresies, envyings, murders, drunkenness, orgies, and things like these; of which I forewarn you, even as I also forewarned you, that those who practice such things will not inherit the Kingdom of God. But the fruit of the Spirit is love, joy, peace, patience, kindness, goodness, faith, gentleness, and self-control. Against such things there is no law." (Gal. 5:19-23)

Ephesians

In his letter to the church at Ephesus in Asia Minor (now modern-day Turkey) the Apostle Paul reminded the Ephesian believers, "You were not born Jewish. . . . Remember that in the past you were without Christ. You were not citizens of Israel, and you had no part in the agreements with the promise that God made to his people. You had no hope, and you did not know God. But now in Christ Jesus, you who were far away from God are brought near . . ." (Eph. 2:11-13 NCV)

Much of this letter is devoted to reminding us how to live as followers of Jesus. Paul addresses advice to wives and husbands, to children and parents, to slaves and masters, and to all believers. We all have a struggle against invisible enemies, and Paul advises us how to prepare for that struggle as if putting on a suit of armor:

"Put on the full armor of God so that you can fight against the devil's evil tricks. Our fight is not against people on earth but against the rulers and authorities and the powers of this world's darkness, against the spiritual powers of evil in the heavenly world. That is why you need to put on God's full armor. Then on the day of evil you will be able to stand strong. And when you have finished the whole fight, you will still be standing. So stand strong, with the belt of truth tied around your waist and the protection of right living on your chest. On your feet wear the Good News of peace to help you stand strong. And also use the shield of faith with which you can stop all the burning arrows of the

Evil One. Accept God's salvation as your helmet, and take the sword of the Spirit, which is the word of God." (Eph. 6:11-17 NCV)

Philippians

When Paul wrote his letter to the church at Philippi he was "in prison because I am a believer in Christ." (Phil. 1:13 NCV) Paul's words and experiences serve as an encouragement to followers of Jesus today who face imprisonment or worse in many parts of the earth.

He urged Christians, "Do everything without complaining or arguing. Then you will be innocent and without any wrong. You will be God's children without fault. But you are living with crooked and mean people all around you, among whom you shine like stars in the dark world. You offer the teaching that gives life." (Phil. 2:14-16 NCV) "Do not worry about anything, but pray and ask God for everything you need, always giving thanks. And God's peace, which is so great we cannot understand it, will keep your hearts and minds in Christ Jesus." (Phil. 4:6-7 NCV)

Colossians

In his letter to the Colossian congregation Paul addressed theological matters, declaring here that Jesus "is the image of the invisible God, the firstborn of all creation. For by him all things were created, in the heavens and on the earth, things visible and things invisible, whether thrones or dominions or principalities or powers; all things have been created through him, and for him. He is before all things, and in him all things are held together. He is the head of the body, the assembly, who is the beginning, the firstborn from the dead; that in all things he might have the preeminence. For all the fullness was pleased to dwell in him; and through him to reconcile all things to himself, by him, whether things on the earth, or things in the heavens, having made peace through the blood of his cross." (Col. 1:15-19) And he added, "For in him all the fullness of the Godhead dwells bodily." (Col. 2:9)

Paul also reminded the Colossian believers that they were not obligated to follow the ceremonial laws given through Moses, which prefigured or pointed forward to things that were fulfilled in Christ: "Therefore do not let anyone judge you by what you eat or drink, or with regard to a religious festival, a New Moon celebration or a Sabbath day. These are a shadow of the things that were to come; the reality, however, is found in Christ." (Col. 2:16-17 NIV)

We can see from his conclusion, that Paul intended his letters to be circulated among the churches: "After this letter has been read to you, see that it is also read in the church of the Laodiceans and that you in turn read the letter from Laodicea." (Col. 4:16 NIV)

1 and 2 Thessalonians

Paul commended the believers in Thessalonica because, "when you received the word of God, which you heard from us, you accepted it not as the word of men, but as it actually is, the word of God, which is at work in you who believe." (1 Thess. 2:13 NIV)

He also reminded them that, "God wants you to be holy and to stay away from sexual sins. . . . Don't use your body for sexual sin like the people who do not know God. Also, do not wrong or cheat another Christian in this way. The Lord will punish people who do those things as we have already told you and warned you. God called us to be holy and does not want us to live in sin. So, the person who refuses to obey this teaching is disobeying God, not simply a human teaching." (1 Thess. 4:3-8 NCV)

In both letters to the Thessalonians Paul spoke of the coming return of Christ: "According to the Lord's own word, we tell you that we who are still alive, who are left till the coming of the Lord, will certainly not precede those who have fallen asleep. For the Lord himself will come down from heaven, with a loud command, with the voice of the archangel and with the trumpet call of God, and the dead in Christ will rise first. After that, we who are still alive and are left will be caught up together with them in the clouds to meet the Lord in the air. And so we will be with the Lord forever." (1 Thess. 4:15-17 NIV) "Then he will punish those who do not know God and who do not obey the Good News about our Lord Jesus Christ. Those people will be punished with a destruction that continues forever. They will be kept away from the Lord and from his great power." (2 Thess. 1:8-9 NCV)

1 and 2 Timothy

The Apostle Paul met a younger man named Timothy when he traveled to Derbe and Lystra in Asia Minor (now Turkey). Although his father was evidently a pagan Greek, Timothy's mother was a Jewish Christian, and she had raised Timothy in the faith. Paul took Timothy with him as he continued his missionary journeys. By the time the Apostle wrote these letters to him, Timothy was serving as Paul's representative in Ephesus and other churches they had visited together. "As I urged you when I went into Macedonia, stay there in Ephesus so that you may command certain men not to teach false doctrines any longer." (1 Tim. 1:3 NIV)

By the time he wrote his second letter to Timothy, Paul was nearing the time when he would be martyred for preaching the Gospel. Speaking of the Hebrew Old Testament, Paul reminded Timothy that "from infancy you have known the holy Scriptures, which are able to make you wise for salvation through faith in Christ Jesus." (2 Tim. 3:15 NIV) And he continued, "All Scripture is God-breathed and is useful for teaching, rebuking, correcting and training in righteousness, so that the man of God may be thoroughly equipped for every good work." (2 Tim. 3:16-17 NIV)

Paul's letters encouraged Timothy to remain strong in faith and to set an example for others in good conduct. He also gave Timothy guidelines for overseers and deacons in the churches.

Titus

A disciple the Apostle Paul had introduced to Christianity, Titus traveled with him on his missionary journeys. Paul left Titus "in Crete so you could finish doing the things that still needed to be done and so you could appoint elders in every town, as I directed you." (Tit. 1:5 NCV) The letter includes guidelines for making those appointments, as well as instructions on the right way for believers to live their lives.

Philemon

The Apostle Paul addressed this brief letter to Philemon, a wealthy man Paul had converted to Christianity and whose run-away slave Onesimus was also converted by Paul when he encountered him on his travels. Paul urged Philemon to forgive Onesimus and to allow him to remain with Paul.

Slavery was part of the social fabric of the Roman Empire, enshrined in law, and generally was not as harsh or oppressive as the enslavement of Africans in the American South. Rather than foment revolution in a society where a large percentage of the population worked as slaves, Paul advised believers, "Were you a slave when you were called? Don't let it trouble you—although if you can gain your freedom, do so. For the one who was a slave when called to faith in the Lord is the Lord's freed person; similarly, the one who was free when called is Christ's slave. You were bought at a price; do not become slaves of human beings. Brothers and sisters, each person, as responsible to God, should remain in the situation they were in when God called them." (1 Cor. 7:21-24 NIV) Also, "Masters, provide your slaves with what is right and fair, because you know that you also have a Master in heaven." (Col. 4:1 NIV)

Hebrews

The author of this letter is not named, but church tradition attributes it to the Apostle Paul. It concludes with indications that the writer was in Italy at the time, and was waiting for Timothy to join him before he resumed traveling. (Heb. 13:23-24)

Written to Christian believers, the letter derives its title from the subject matter, which deals primarily with how God's covenant with the Jewish people through Moses prefigured or foreshadowed the new covenant through Jesus. The writer quotes Jeremiah 31:31-34 and many other passages from the Old Testament, explaining how they are fulfilled as prophetic pictures of the Christian arrangement.

It also stresses the importance of faith, which it defines as "assurance of things hoped for, proof of things not seen." (Heb. 11:1) And it outlines how the major personages in the Old Testament exercised faith by trusting and obeying God.

James

Attributed to James the half-brother of Jesus who served as a leader of the church in Jerusalem, this letter addresses the need for Christians to live right. "People who think they are religious but say things they should not say are just fooling themselves. Their 'religion' is worth nothing. Religion that God accepts as pure and without fault is this: caring for orphans or widows who need help, and keeping yourself free from the world's evil influence." (Jas. 1:26-27 NCV)

James speaks of how faith and good works fit together in a Christian's life, and how "faith, if it has no works, is dead in itself." (Jas. 2:17) Just believing that God exists, is nothing to brag about; "the demons believe that, too, and they tremble with fear," James reminds us. (Jas. 2:19 NCV)

He also cautions readers on the dangers of pursuing riches, and the danger of not bridling our tongues and controlling our speech.

1 and 2 Peter

The Apostle Peter's letters encourage Christians to live right and to patiently endure suffering when persecuted for the faith or when living under difficult circumstances. He gives advice to believing women who are married to unbelieving men, and to slaves or servants working for difficult masters. He cites Jesus' example: "People insulted Christ, but he did not insult them in return. Christ suffered, but he did not threaten." (1 Pet. 2:23 NCV)

Peter also assures us that the Bible is truly the word of God, not men. Speaking of the Old Testament, he writes, "Most of all, you must understand this: No prophecy in the Scriptures ever comes from the prophet's own interpretation. No prophecy ever came from what a person wanted to say, but people led by the Holy Spirit spoke words from God." (2 Pet. 1:20-21 NCV) In his second letter Peter also refers to portions of the New Testament that had already been written—the letters of the Apostle Paul—as inspired Scripture.

Peter also devotes a large portion of his second letter to warning against false teachers in the churches, describing them as greedy and immoral. "Those false teachers only want your money, so they will use you by telling you lies." (2 Pet. 2:3 NCV)

But Peter encourages followers of Jesus to keep waiting patiently for God's Judgment Day, which will come even though unbelievers ridicule the idea that Jesus promised to return. "It is important for you to understand what will happen in the last days. People will laugh at you. They will live doing the evil things they want to do. They will say, 'Jesus promised to come again. Where is he? Our fathers have died, but the world continues the way it has been since it was made.' But they do not want to remember what happened long ago" when God executed judgment on the world in Noah's day. (2 Pet. 3:3-5 NCV)

Peter concludes, "You therefore, beloved, knowing these things beforehand, beware, lest being carried away with the error of the wicked, you fall from your own steadfastness. But grow in the grace and knowledge of our Lord and Savior Jesus Christ. To him be the glory both now and forever. Amen." (2 Pet. 3:17-18)

1, 2 and 3 John

Besides the Gospel bearing his name, the Apostle John wrote three letters that are included in the New Testament.

The first letter encourages believers to love one another, and to turn away from sin. "If we say that we have no sin, we deceive ourselves, and the truth is not in us. If we confess our sins, he is faithful and righteous to forgive us the sins, and to cleanse us from all unrighteousness. If we say that we haven't sinned, we make him a liar, and his word is not in us. My little children, I write these things to you so that you may not sin. If anyone sins, we have a Counselor with the Father, Jesus Christ, the righteous. And he is the atoning sacrifice for our sins, and not for ours only, but also for the whole world." (1 John 1:8-2:2)

John's second and third letters are very brief—each just over a dozen verses long. Both warn of enemies inside and outside the churches, a theme also found in the first letter. By the time John wrote his third letter, it appears that some churches were already being taken over by such enemies. He said, "I wrote something to the church; but Diotrephes, who loves to be first among them, does not accept what we say. For this reason, if I come, I will call attention to his deeds which he does, unjustly accusing us with wicked words; and not satisfied with this, he himself does not receive the brethren, either, and he forbids those who desire to do so and puts them out of the church." (3 John 9-10 NASB)

Jude

Like John's second and third letters, Jude's letter is also very brief, just two dozen verses. The disciple tells Christian readers, "I wanted very much to write you about the salvation we all share. But I felt the need to write you about something else: I want to encourage you to fight hard for the faith that was given the holy people of God once and for all time. Some people have secretly entered your group. . . . They are against God and have changed the grace of our God into a reason for sexual sin." (Jude 3-4)

This is a common thread found in many of the letters of the Apostles in the New Testament—that God's grace and mercy must not be used as a pretext for persisting in sexual sin. Jude goes on to remind readers that "Sodom and Gomorrah, and the cities around them, having . . . given themselves over to sexual immorality and gone after strange flesh, are set forth as an example, suffering the punishment of eternal fire." (Jude 7)

Revelation (also called Apocalypse)

Quite different from the other books of the New Testament, and somewhat reminiscent of the visions recorded by the Old Testament prophets, "This is the Revelation of Jesus Christ, which God gave him to show to his servants the things which must happen soon, which he sent and made known by his angel to his servant, John, who testified to God's word, and of the testimony of Jesus Christ, about everything that he saw." (Rev. 1:1-2) John is told, "What you see, write in a book and send to the seven assemblies: to Ephesus, Smyrna, Pergamum, Thyatira, Sardis, Philadelphia, and to Laodicea." (Rev. 1:11)

John then sees a vision of the risen Christ, who gives him specific messages to each of these seven prominent Christian churches in ancient Asia Minor. Jesus commends the church in Ephesus for "your toil and perseverance, and that you can't tolerate evil men, and have tested those who call themselves apostles, and they are not, and found them false" and "that you hate the works of the Nicolaitans, which I also hate." (Rev. 2:2, 6) But Jesus also warns them, "I have this against you, that you left your first love. Remember therefore from where you have fallen, and repent and do the first works; or else I am coming to you swiftly, and will move your lampstand out of its place, unless you repent." (Rev. 2:4-5)

Jesus calls five of the seven churches to "repent" for straying, in various ways, from following him.

The remainder of the book of Revelation presents a long series of visions full of signs and symbols: "A great and wondrous sign appeared in heaven" (12:1 NIV), "Then another sign appeared in heaven" (12:3 NIV), "And I saw another sign in heaven" (15:1 KJV) The exact meanings of these signs and symbols have been the subject of debate for centuries, but the basic overall message is clear: God will intervene in human affairs to put an end to man's governments and to establish the worldwide rule of the Kingdom of God. In the process, God sends one plague or disaster after another—diseases, scorching heat, pollution of the seas and rivers, destruction of "a third of the trees" (Rev. 8:7 NCV), and so on—to punish rebellious mankind and call people to repent. "The other people who were not killed by these terrible disasters still did not change their hearts . . . and turn away from murder or evil magic, from their sexual sins or stealing." (Rev. 9:20-21 NCV)

The Revelation goes on to show the world's governments and armies suffering defeat at a "place that is called Armageddon in the Hebrew language" (Rev. 16:16 NCV), after which Christ rules for a thousand years.

Your service to God

When Jesus calls us to follow him, he calls us to a life of service. Jesus himself set the example. He came from his Father's throne in heaven, entitled to receive worship and obedience from humans . . .

"when he brings in the firstborn into the world he says, 'Let all the angels of God worship him.'" —Hebrews 1:6

. . . but he put aside his glory, humbled himself and served others, setting an example for us to follow.

"Have this in your mind, which was also in Christ Jesus, who, existing in the form of God, didn't consider equality with God a thing to be grasped, but emptied himself, taking the form of a servant, being made in the likeness of men. And being found in human form, he humbled himself, becoming obedient to death, yes, the death of the cross." —Philippians 2:5-8

Should we shrink back from some humble form of service God may call us to? During the years before embarking on his three-year ministry of preaching and working miracles, Jesus evidently worked for years in his foster father Joseph's carpentry shop. How could we think ourselves above menial tasks, when Jesus was even willing to do a household servant's job, washing the feet of his disciples?

"Jesus, knowing that the Father had given all things into his hands, and that he came forth from God, and was going to God, arose from supper, and laid aside his outer garments. He took a towel, and wrapped a towel around his waist. Then he poured water into the basin, and began to wash the disciples' feet, and to wipe them with the towel that was wrapped around him. . . . he said to them, '. . . If I then, the Lord and the Teacher, have washed your feet, you also ought to wash one another's feet.'" —John 13:3-5, 12, 14

So, in our church or place of Christian fellowship, we should gladly accept any service that God may call on us to perform. There are many ways to help in the church. Paul wrote,

"And in the church God has appointed first of all apostles, second prophets, third teachers, then workers of miracles, also those having gifts of healing, those able to help others, those with gifts of administration, and those speaking in different kinds of tongues."

—1 Corinthians 12:28 NIV

One Christian woman cited as a good example was Tabitha or Dorcas, whom the Apostle Peter resurrected after she fell sick and died. She was in the habit of making articles of clothing and giving them to poor widows who, in ancient Roman society, struggled to survive, depending on the charity of others:

"**Now there was at Joppa a certain disciple named Tabitha, which when translated, means Dorcas. This woman was full of good works and acts of mercy which she did. It happened in those days that she fell sick, and died. When they had washed her, they laid her in an upper room. As Lydda was near Joppa, the disciples, hearing that Peter was there, sent two men to him, imploring him not to delay in coming to them. Peter got up and went with them. When he had come, they brought him into the upper room. All the widows stood by him weeping, and showing the coats and garments which Dorcas had made while she was with them.**"

—Acts 9:36-39

Jesus views such good works and acts of mercy done to his followers as if they were done to him personally:

"'". . . **I was hungry, and you gave me food to eat. I was thirsty, and you gave me drink. I was a stranger, and you took me in. I was naked, and you clothed me. I was sick, and you visited me. I was in prison, and you came to me.**"

"'. . . "**Lord, when did we see you hungry, and feed you; or thirsty, and give you a drink? When did we see you as a stranger, and take you in; or naked, and clothe you? When did we see you sick, or in prison, and come to you?**"

"'. . . "**Most certainly I tell you, inasmuch as you did it to one of the least of these my brothers, you did it to me.**"'" —Matthew 25:35-40

Such good works and acts of service do not earn us our salvation, of course—salvation is a free gift from God through Jesus Christ—nor do they offset sinful conduct. Jesus warned that those who persist in sinning and doing evil will not be able to claim entrance into heaven by citing their service to God:

"'**Not every one who says to me, "Lord, Lord," shall enter the kingdom of heaven, but he who does the will of my Father who is in heaven. On that day many will say to me, "Lord, Lord, did we not prophesy in your name, and cast out demons in your name, and do many mighty works in your name?" And then will I declare to them, "I never knew you; depart from me, you evildoers."**'"

—Matthew 7:21-23 RSV

Good works of Christian service do not earn us our salvation, but rather when God gives us the free gift of salvation it is our duty to respond by doing good:

"For we are God's workmanship, created in Christ Jesus to do good works, which God prepared in advance for us to do."

—Ephesians 2:10 NIV

So, as followers of Jesus we have a responsibility to do good works—it is expected of us.

One of the greatest works is to carry out the great commission of bringing the Gospel message to others. Before ascending to heaven, Jesus said,

"'Go, and make disciples of all nations, baptizing them in the name of the Father and of the Son and of the Holy Spirit, teaching them to observe all things that I commanded you.'"

—Matthew 28:19-20

We may not all be called to be teachers or evangelizers, but we can all tell others what Jesus has done for us—our personal testimony of being saved from our sins and having our lives turned around by our Lord and Savior. After healing a man and rescuing him from a terrible life,

"Jesus sent him away, saying, 'Return to your house, and declare what great things God has done for you.' He went his way, proclaiming throughout the whole city what great things Jesus had done for him." —Luke 8:38-39

We can do the same when relatives or work mates or neighbors notice that we have changed after becoming followers of Jesus. We can tell them what Jesus has done for us, and thus introduce them to the Gospel message.

"Jezebel" in the churches

To the Christian church in the ancient city of Thyatira the resurrected and risen Christ sent this message:

"I have this against you: You tolerate that woman Jezebel, who calls herself a prophetess. By her teaching she misleads my servants into sexual immorality and the eating of food sacrificed to idols. I have given her time to repent of her immorality, but she is unwilling. So I will cast her on a bed of suffering, and I will make those who commit adultery with her suffer intensely, unless they repent of her ways. I will strike her children dead. Then all the churches will know that I am he who searches hearts and minds, and I will repay each of you according to your deeds."

—Revelation 2:20-23 NIV

Similarly, the early disciple Jude said that he wanted to write a letter about the salvation Christians share, but instead he had to write a warning about false teachers who were bringing sexual immorality and all sorts of other wrong practices into the churches:

"Dear friends, although I was very eager to write to you about the salvation we share, I felt I had to write and urge you to contend for the faith that was once for all entrusted to the saints.

"For certain men whose condemnation was written about long ago have secretly slipped in among you. They are godless men, who change the grace of our God into a license for immorality and deny Jesus Christ our only Sovereign and Lord." —Jude 3-4

Although Jude wanted to write to the churches about the salvation we share as believers, he felt led by God's Spirit to write instead a warning against certain men who had slipped into the churches to mislead them into sin.

Similarly, I would prefer to write a positive message here about the joy of following Jesus and the good things found in Christian churches, but I am forced to include also a strong warning against the modern acceptance of sexual sin and other pagan practices in many churches. The modern Jezebels who have brought such things into today's churches are just as unacceptable to Jesus as the Jezebel he condemned in his message to the church in Thyatira.

That message in the book of Revelation condemned Jezebel for misleading Christians "into sexual immorality and the eating of food sacrificed to idols." Has anyone actually introduced anything comparable to eating food sacrificed to idols in today's churches?

Yes—through the practice of meditation associated with non-Christian religions from the East. Although the actual idols found in Hindu temples may not have been brought into Christian churches, the practices Hindus employ to worship those idols have been brought in.

Several decades ago the promoters of Hinduism in India saw that their religion was not very appealing to people in the West, so they came up with some ways to disguise it, and to get Hindu religious practices to be accepted by Europeans and Americans—without calling it Hinduism.

They came up with two ways to disguise their worship and get Western Christians to accept it: by presenting Hindu religious practices as physical exercises and as relaxing meditation.

Hindu meditation was introduced to America several decades ago by a south Asian who used the title "Yogi" after his name. He presented it, not as religion, but as a "relaxation technique." People would be taught to relax by repeating some meaningless sounds called Mantras—emptying their minds, and relaxing, repeating the Mantras over and over again, thinking about nothing but the Mantra. The campaign to introduce this practice was successful. The result was that this form of meditation was adopted everywhere, from large business corporations that wanted to make their workers more productive, to Christian churches.

But the problem is that Mantras are not just meaningless sounds; they are elements of Hindu prayer. And a Yogi is not just a teacher of relaxation techniques. As of this writing, the article on "Mantra" in the Wikipedia (the free online encyclopedia found on the web at wikipedia.org) says mantras "originated in the Vedic tradition of India, later becoming an essential part of the Hindu tradition and a customary practice within Buddhism, Sikhism, and Jainism. The use of mantras is now widespread throughout various spiritual movements which are based on, or off-shoots of, the practices in the earlier Eastern traditions and religions. . . . For the authors of the Hindu scriptures of the Upanishads, the syllable Aum, itself constituting a mantra, represents Brahman, the godhead, as well as the whole of creation. . . . While praying by reciting this mantra, the devotee bows with respect to Arihantas, Siddhas, spiritual leaders (Acharyas), teachers (Upadyayas) and all the monks."

The Wikipedia says this concerning the title Yogi, "the word Yogi is also generically used to refer to both male and female practitioners of yoga and related meditative practices in Buddhism, Jainism, Taoism etc. . . . In Hinduism the term refers to an adherent of Yoga. As an Urdu term, yogi . . . is mostly used to refer to wandering Sufi saints and ascetics. The word is also often used in the Buddhist context to describe Buddhist monks or a householder devoted to meditation." The article then concludes with a "List of Yogis . . . List of Hindu gurus and saints."

So, Eastern meditation—particularly when a mantra is recited—is clearly an element of non-Christian religion. It has no place in the lives of Christians. For some people, the practice of Eastern meditation does not go beyond repeating Hindu prayers, but for others it leads to personality changes and deeper involvement in forms of worship of other gods—false worship that is hostile to Jesus Christ and condemned in the Bible.

But I mentioned that there were two ways that Hindus found to disguise their worship and get Westerners to practice it. Hindu meditation under a different name was one of the disguises. The other disguise that Hindu worship adopted was Yoga. And this disguised form of Eastern religion, too, has been widely adopted by many people in the West. Large business corporations commonly invite employees to take Yoga classes. And Yoga classes are found in many churches, sometimes taught by the pastor or his wife.

But, according to any dictionary or encyclopedia, the word Yoga is associated with meditative practices in Hinduism. The major branches of Yoga within the Hindu religion are Ra-ja Yoga, Karma Yoga, Jnana Yoga, Bhakti Yoga, and Hatha Yoga, and someone who practices Yoga to a high level of attainment is called a Yogi.

Some try to claim that Yoga is just stretching exercises, nothing more. But many of the postures assumed during those exercises are positions of worship for various Hindu gods. The goal of Yoga is not just to affect the body, but also to affect the mind. People who become serious about Yoga may easily pass beyond stretching their body and find themselves taking on the teachings of the Hindu religion—a polytheistic, idol-worshipping religion which is hostile to the Gospel of Jesus Christ.

Another element of idolatry or pagan religion brought into Christian churches by modern Jezebels (male and female) involves the practice of spiritism, witchcraft or sorcery.

The society we live in today uses all the media at its disposal to teach us to view sorcerers or practicers of witchcraft as harmless, or even as good. Sorcerers are even presented as heroes we should want to imitate. This has been going on for decades, but has reached a new peak in this generation. I recall as a youngster seeing the Walt Disney movie *The Sorcerer's Apprentice*. It seemed harmless enough, but served as a wedge to open the door to more serious endeavors. Today's young people have been bombarded with a series of Harry Potter books and movies promoting sorcery in a way never seen before.

Witchcraft and spiritism used to hide out in dark places, but today they have exploded into the open. We see palm readers and tarot card readers everywhere. Instead of just a physical massage, massage parlors are offering Reiki, a Buddhist spiritual practice that claims to transfer spiritual energy through the hands of the practitioner. Many people are decorating their front yards for Halloween the way they used to decorate only for Christmas.

What does God Almighty say about sorcery, witchcraft and spiritism? It's God's opinion that counts in these matters, not our opinion or our neighbor's opinion. And it's in the inspired Word of God, the Bible, that we find God's viewpoint expressed.

Notice what God said about sorcerers, as recorded by the Hebrew prophet Malachi:

"'So I will come near to you for judgment. I will be quick to testify against sorcerers, adulterers and perjurers, against those who defraud labourers of their wages, who oppress the widows and the fatherless, and deprive aliens of justice, but do not fear me,' says the LORD Almighty." —Malachi 3:5 NIV

So, God groups sorcery in with adultery, perjury, fraud and injustice. Now, turning from the Old Testament to the New Testament, notice what the Apostle Paul wrote to the church in Galatia about those who practice witchcraft:

"The acts of the sinful nature are obvious: sexual immorality, impurity and debauchery; idolatry and witchcraft; hatred, discord, jealousy, fits of rage, selfish ambition, dissensions, factions and envy; drunkenness, orgies and the like, I warn you, as I did before, that those who live like this will not inherit the kingdom of God."

—Galatians 5:19-21 NIV

The Bible book of Revelation contains similar strong warnings against those who practice magic arts:

"But the cowardly, the unbelieving, the vile, the murderers, the sexually immoral, those who practise magic arts, the idolaters and all liars—their place will be in the fiery lake of burning sulphur. This is the second death." —Revelation 21:8 NIV

"Outside are the dogs, those who practise magic arts, the sexually immoral, the murderers, the idolaters and everyone who loves and practises falsehood." —Revelation 22:15 NIV

So, people who "practice magic arts" end up receiving the same judgment from God as murderers and worshipers of idols. What if you have been involved in such practices? Is there any hope for you? Yes, by putting faith in Jesus Christ, you can be set free, and can be forgiven for all your sins. Jesus will help you put the sin of sorcery behind you, and will help you learn His righteous ways of living. When the first century Apostles of Christ went preaching the Gospel throughout pre-Christian Europe and Asia, they encountered many pagans who practiced magic, witchcraft and sorcery. Acts 19:19-20 tells us what these people did when they became Christian believers:

"A number who had practiced sorcery brought their scrolls together and burned them publicly. When they calculated the value of the scrolls, the total came to fifty thousand drachmas. In this way the word of the Lord spread widely and grew in power."

—Acts 19:19-20

When people who used to practice sorcery learned about Jesus and put faith in him, they quit practicing magic, witchcraft and sorcery. In fact, they publicly burned their books on sorcery. Sorcery, witchcraft and magic are not acceptable among true Christians. Those who have been involved in such practices need to follow the example just quoted from the Bible book of Acts— not bring such practices into the church, no matter how well accepted they may be in the surrounding community.

Besides things related to pagan idolatry, the book of Revelation says Jezebel also brought sexual immorality into the church. She was living up to the behavior of her namesake in ancient Israel, the pagan mother of king Joram,

"'And when Joram saw Jehu, he said, "Is it peace, Jehu?" He answered, "What peace can there be, so long as the whorings and the sorceries of your mother Jezebel are so many?"'

—2 Kings 9:22 English Standard Version

(To better understand why Revelation uses the name Jezebel, you may wish to read about that original Jezebel in the Old Testament in 1Kings chapter 16 through 2 Kings chapter 9.)

The men condemned in the opening verses of Jude's letter likewise brought sexual misconduct into the church, changing "the grace of our God into a license for immorality." (Jude 4) Do we see something similar in churches today?

Over the course of the past hundred years or so, there has been a dramatic change in the popular view of sexual morality and what is considered right and wrong. Behavior that was once viewed as sinful and bad is now accepted as normal and good. People who once would have been shunned as gross sinners are now held up before the public as role models and heroes. Whereas people who practiced what the Bible classifies as sexual misconduct used to be condemned in the public media, today the media treat such people as celebrities. Christians who uphold the Bible's standards of right and wrong are often presented today as old fashioned, out of step with the times, intolerant, homophobic or guilty of 'hate speech' or 'hate crimes.'

Pressured to conform to this new popular trend to view all sorts of sexual misconduct as morally acceptable, many churches have made a similar about-face, now accepting into membership and even ordaining as clergy, people whose behavior would have disqualified them in past generations.

Has God really changed his mind on sexual morality? How should you view churches that welcome as members and clergy people whose behavior is condemned by the Bible?

The ancient pre-Christian pagan world often tolerated and accepted conduct that did not meet with God's approval, and so back in the first century there was a danger that the community's attitudes might be carried into the newly formed churches as pagans were converted and embraced Christianity. To keep that from happening, the Apostle Paul wrote this to the church in ancient Rome:

"Do not conform any longer to the pattern of this world, but be transformed by the renewing of your mind. Then you will be able to test and approve what God's will is—his good, pleasing and perfect will." —Romans 12:2

Paul's words "Do not conform any longer to the pattern of this world" are rendered with this paraphrase in the J. B. Phillips translation:

"Don't let the world around you squeeze you into its own mould."

So, even though today's new non-biblical views and attitudes may be widely accepted in our community and our nation, we need to struggle not to let the world around us squeeze us into its mold.

And the world is actively trying to do that. No matter where we turn in the media today—radio, television, newspapers and magazines, the internet—we are bombarded with images and messages saying that all sorts of expressions of sexuality are okay, good and acceptable, and that those who uphold the Bible's standards of morality are the ones who are wrong. It is clear that the world around us is trying as hard as it can to squeeze everyone into this mold.

What does the Bible actually say on these matters?

The Bible begins talking about sexual morality way back in the book of Genesis, the first book of the Bible, and it keeps referring to this subject all the way through the Revelation or Apocalypse, the last book of the New Testament.

In its second chapter, the book of Genesis states,

"Then the LORD God said, 'It is not good for the man to be alone. I will make a helper who is right for him.'" —Genesis 2:18 NCV

So, God created the first woman and gave her to the first man in marriage:

"So a man will leave his father and mother and be united with his wife, and the two will become one body." —Genesis 2:24 NCV

This was meant to serve as a pattern for all mankind, and it did indeed serve as a pattern that people have followed down through history. But many men, even those whose lives are recorded in the Bible, chose to take multiple wives.

The Bible record shows how polygamy brought conflict, grief and unhappiness to those who practiced it. (Gen. 30:1-2, 14-16; 1 Sam. 1:3-8) When God gave the nation of Israel more than six hundred laws through Moses, he regulated the practices of divorce and polygamy—limiting them at that time, without putting a stop to them. Jesus explained it this way when Jewish religious leaders asked him about men divorcing their wives: "Why then did Moses command us to give her a bill of divorce, and divorce her?" Jesus replied:

"'Moses, because of the hardness of your hearts, allowed you to divorce your wives, but from the beginning it has not been so. I tell you that whoever divorces his wife, except for sexual immorality, and marries another, commits adultery; and he who marries her when she is divorced commits adultery.'"

—Matthew 19:8-9

Jesus referred back to the first marriage in Genesis as the pattern God intended for mankind to follow:

"'Haven't you read that he who made them from the beginning made them male and female, and said, "For this cause a man shall leave his father and mother, and shall join to his wife; and the two shall become one flesh?" So that they are no more two, but one flesh. What therefore God has joined together, don't let man tear apart.'"
—Matthew 19:4-6

And when Christian churches were being established in a world that still practiced polygamy and divorce, the higher standard of monogamous marriage was held up as the example to follow, and a requirement for church leaders:

"This is a faithful saying: if a man seeks the office of an overseer, he desires a good work. The overseer therefore must be without reproach, the husband of one wife" —1 Timothy 3:1-2

But most of mankind has been in rebellion against God throughout the history of this planet. An outstanding case was recorded in the book of Genesis:

"Now the men of Sodom were wicked and were sinning greatly against the LORD." —Genesis 13:13 NIV

"Because the outcry against Sodom and Gomorrah is great, and because their sin is very grave," God considered destroying those cities. But first he sent two angels in the form of men to investigate, and he discussed the matter with Abraham. Abraham begged God not to "destroy the righteous with the wicked," and God agreed that he would spare the whole city of Sodom if he found ten good people there. (Gen. 18:17-32 NKJV)

Part of Abraham's concern must have been due to the fact that his nephew Lot was then living in Sodom. In fact, when the investigating angels arrived that evening, Lot invited them to spend the night at his house.

"But before they lay down, the men of the city, the men of Sodom, surrounded the house, both young and old, all the people from every quarter. They called to Lot, and said to him, 'Where are the men who came in to you this night? Bring them out to us, that we may have sex with them.'" —Genesis 19:4-5

The angels did not find ten righteous people in the city. Instead they led out Lot and his immediate family, so that God could destroy the place, and

"Then the LORD rained upon Sodom and upon Gomorrah brimstone and fire from the LORD out of heaven; And he overthrew those cities, and all the plain, and all the inhabitants of the cities, and that which grew upon the ground." —Genesis 19:24-25 KJV

Our modern English words 'sodomy' and 'sodomize' come from the name of that ancient city of Sodom that God destroyed as punishment for its inhabitants' sins.

Several centuries later when God led the people of Israel out of Egypt and into the Promised Land and gave them laws to live by, these laws included many that spelled out what God declared to be right and wrong in regard to sexual relations.

"'You must never have sexual relations with your close relatives . . . You must not have sexual relations with your brother's wife . . . You must not have sexual relations with your neighbor's wife . . . You must not have sexual relations with a man as you would a woman. That is a hateful sin. You must not have sexual relations with an animal; it is not natural.'" —Leviticus 18:6, 16, 20, 22-23 NCV

These moral laws given through Moses in the Old Testament were for the Jewish nation: "'These rules are for the citizens of Israel and for the people who live with you.'" (Leviticus 18:21 NCV) Although Christians are not under the ceremonial law that required animal sacrifices pointing forward to Jesus' sacrificial death, and that required Jews to follow a special kosher diet and to dress differently to keep them separate from non-Jews, we can still learn God's will from the moral law that expresses God's unchangeable declarations of what is right and wrong. Notice how the Apostle Paul points this out:

"But we know that the law is good, if a man uses it lawfully, as knowing this, that law is not made for a righteous man, but for the lawless and insubordinate, for the ungodly and sinners, for the unholy and profane, for murderers of fathers and murderers of mothers, for manslayers, for the sexually immoral, for

homosexuals, for slave-traders, for liars, for perjurers, and for any other thing contrary to the sound doctrine; according to the Good News of the glory of the blessed God, which was committed to my trust.

"And I thank him who enabled me, Christ Jesus our Lord, because he counted me faithful, appointing me to service; although I was before a blasphemer, a persecutor, and insolent. However, I obtained mercy, because I did it ignorantly in unbelief."

—1 Timothy:1 8-13

Like Paul, we too may have sinned "ignorantly in unbelief," but we too can obtain God's mercy when we repent and choose to follow Jesus in these matters. Like Paul, we too can change our conduct, abandoning practices that God condemns. Jesus is alive and active in the lives of those who accept him not only as their Savior, but also as their Lord—to save them from their sins and to lead them through life from now on. God's Holy Spirit can empower believers to make changes in their conduct that would have been impossible on their own. As ancient king David wrote, we can pray,

"LORD . . . Take away my desire to do evil or to join others in doing wrong. Don't let me eat tasty food with those who do evil."

—Psalm 141:4 NCV

As we read the New Testament, we find that the Apostles and disciples of Jesus uphold God's same moral standard as expressed in the moral law given to the Jews, and they warn us that God will execute the same sort of punishment again against those who persist in practicing sexual immorality, as he did in the Old Testament—even referring back to God's destruction of Sodom and Gomorrah as an example. The Apostle Peter writes that God

"condemned the cities of Sodom and Gomorrah by burning them to ashes, and made them an example of what is going to happen to the ungodly." —2 Peter 2:6 NIV

The disciple Jude writes similarly at Jude 7, pointing out clearly the sexual nature of their sins:

"In a similar way, Sodom and Gomorrah and the surrounding towns gave themselves up to sexual immorality and perversion. They serve as an example of those who suffer the punishment of eternal fire." —Jude 7 NIV

Like the Old Testament, the Christian New Testament plainly spells out the conduct God condemns:

"Therefore God also gave them up in the lusts of their hearts to uncleanness, that their bodies should be dishonored among themselves, who exchanged the truth of God for a lie, and worshiped and served the creature rather than the Creator, who is blessed forever. Amen.

"For this reason, God gave them up to vile passions. For their women changed the natural function into that which is against nature.

"Likewise also the men, leaving the natural function of the woman, burned in their lust toward one another, men doing what is inappropriate with men, and receiving in themselves the due penalty of their error.

"Even as they refused to have God in their knowledge, God gave them up to a reprobate mind, to do those things which are not fitting; being filled with all unrighteousness, sexual immorality, wickedness, covetousness . . . who, knowing the ordinance of God, that those who practice such things are worthy of death, not only do the same, but also approve of those who practice them."

—Romans 1:24-32

Notice that this passage closes by condemning, not only those who practice such things, but also those who "approve of those who practice them."

But what about the popular notion today that people who practice these things are 'born that way'—that God even made them that way—and so it is okay for them to behave that way? Yes, people are born with the desire to sin, but that does not make it okay to act out those desires. The Bible explains where these sinful desires really come from:

"sin entered into the world through one man, and death through sin; and so death passed to all men, because all sinned. . . . death reigned from Adam until Moses, even over those whose sins weren't like Adam's disobedience." —Romans 5:12-14

As a result of our sinful inheritance from the first man Adam,

"the imagination of man's heart is evil from his youth" —Genesis 8:21

So, the Bible explains that the first man Adam brought sin into the world, and Adam passed on to all of his offspring a tendency to sin: For some people it is a tendency to steal. Other people inherited a tendency toward violence. For some men, it is a very strong desire to be a womanizer; they have a sexual inclination toward multiple women, instead of just one wife. Some have a strong inclination toward homosexual relations. Some people inherited a tendency toward dependence on alcohol or drugs.

Does that mean we should all feel free to act out our sinful inclinations? Of course not. We all need to struggle against inherited sin, no matter what sinful inclination is strongest in our particular case. The Apostle Paul explains it this way:

"No temptation has taken you except what is common to man. God is faithful, who will not allow you to be tempted above what you are able, but will with the temptation also make the way of escape, that you may be able to endure it." —1 Corinthians 10:13

So, if you're struggling with sexual desires—desires to behave in ways that God declares unacceptable—you should not feel condemned. All of us have inherited strong tendencies to sin in one way or another. Rather, you should feel encouraged to keep up the battle against temptation.

We all have struggles against temptations to sin in one form or another. Even the Apostle Paul wrote concerning himself:

"I beat my body and make it my slave so that after I have preached to others, I myself will not be disqualified for the prize."

—1 Corinthians 9:27 NIV

So, even the Apostle Paul struggled against the tendency to sin in his own body. And the Christians that Paul addressed his letters to back in the first century had similar struggles. They, too, like all of us, had inherited sinful tendencies, and many of them had been in the habit of acting out those tendencies through sinful conduct before coming to Jesus for forgiveness of their sins and changing their conduct to obey him as his followers. They stopped their sinful practices and they were washed clean from their sins in the blood of Jesus Christ. Notice what Paul wrote about the particular sins that members of the Corinthian congregation had been practicing before they repented and began following Jesus:

"Or don't you know that the unrighteous will not inherit the Kingdom of God? Don't be deceived. Neither the sexually immoral, nor idolaters, nor adulterers, nor male prostitutes, nor homosexuals, nor thieves, nor covetous, nor drunkards, nor slanderers, nor extortioners, will inherit the Kingdom of God.

"Such were some of you, but you were washed. But you were sanctified. But you were justified in the name of the Lord Jesus, and in the Spirit of our God." —1 Corinthians 6:9-11

Yes, when Paul lists the former sins of the Corinthians, he includes adulterers and male prostitutes and homosexuals, and he confirms that this is what some of them were—not still are, but were, in the past. They had put their sins behind them and were washed clean through their faith in Jesus.

That is quite different from continuing in sin, and bringing that sin into the Church. "Don't be deceived," Paul wrote above. In many churches there are false teachers like Jezebel who deceive their listeners into thinking it is okay to persist in sinful sexual behavior while calling oneself a Christian. That is why Paul listed the above sins and added, "Do not be deceived."

When Jesus healed a man at the pool of Bethesda, he told the man,

"Stop sinning, or something worse may happen to you."

—John 5:14 NIV

The Apostle Paul elaborated on the need to stop sinning in his letter to the congregation in Rome:

"What shall we say, then? Shall we go on sinning so that grace may increase? By no means! We died to sin; how can we live in it any longer? Or don't you know that all of us who were baptized into Christ Jesus were baptized into his death? We were therefore buried with him through baptism into death in order that, just as Christ was raised from the dead through the glory of the Father, we too may live a new life.

" . . . For we know that our old self was crucified with him so that the body of sin might be done away with, that we should no longer be slaves to sin—because anyone who has died has been freed from sin.

"Now if we died with Christ, we believe that we will also live with him. . . .

"In the same way, count yourselves dead to sin but alive to God in Christ Jesus. Therefore do not let sin reign in your mortal body so that you obey its evil desires. Do not offer the parts of your body to sin, as instruments of wickedness, but rather offer yourselves to God, as those who have been brought from death to life; and offer the parts of your body to him as instruments of righteousness. For sin shall not be your master, because you are not under law, but under grace." —Romans 6:1-14 NIV

But today, there are those who teach that sexual misconduct is not sin at all, but that it's okay to practice it. This is again reminiscent of the woman Jezebel in the book of Revelation. The risen Christ says to the church in Thyatira,

"I have this against you: You tolerate that woman Jezebel, who calls herself a prophetess. By her teaching she misleads my servants into sexual immorality." —Revelation 2:20

Yes, this is a teaching in many churches today—that the sexual practices labeled as sin in the Bible have somehow now become acceptable to God. Some of these churches hang a banner on the walls of the church saying, "God is still speaking." And what they mean is that God is now speaking something contrary to what he says throughout the whole Bible from Genesis to Revelation. Obviously it is not the God of the Bible that they are listening to. Obviously they are not following the real Jesus, the Jesus of the Bible.

Of course, much of the world around us today openly dismisses both God and the Bible.

As the Apostle Peter writes,

"in the last days there will come men who scoff at religion and live self-indulgent lives" —2 Peter 3:3 NEB

And then Peter added,

"But the Day of the Lord will come . . ." —2 Peter 3:10

Yes, the day of the Lord will come. Amen! Come, Lord Jesus!

Meanwhile, followers of Jesus must heed the message he gave to the church in Thyatira

"I have this against you: You tolerate that woman Jezebel, who calls herself a prophetess. By her teaching she misleads my servants into sexual immorality and the eating of food sacrificed to idols. I have given her time to repent of her immorality, but she is unwilling. So I will cast her on a bed of suffering, and I will make those who commit adultery with her suffer intensely, unless they repent of her ways. I will strike her children dead. Then all the churches will know that I am he who searches hearts and minds, and I will repay each of you according to your deeds."

—Revelation 2:20-23 NIV

"If we deliberately keep on sinning . . ."

The following passages are so clear about what happens if we deliberately keep on sinning, that I will present them here without any commentary of my own. (Otherwise, someone will accuse me of misinterpreting them.) These scriptures speak for themselves, and need no interpretation.

"If we deliberately keep on sinning after we have received the knowledge of the truth, no sacrifice for sins is left, but only a fearful expectation of judgment and of raging fire that will consume the enemies of God. Anyone who rejected the law of Moses died without mercy on the testimony of two or three witnesses. How much more severely do you think a man deserves to be punished who has trampled the Son of God under foot, who has treated as an unholy thing the blood of the covenant that sanctified him, and who has insulted the Spirit of grace? For we know him who said, 'It is mine to avenge; I will repay,' and again, 'The Lord will judge his people.' It is a dreadful thing to fall into the hands of the living God."
                                                    —Hebrews 10:26-30 NIV

"Brothers, if someone is caught in a sin, you who are spiritual should restore him gently. But watch yourself, or you also may be tempted. . . . Do not be deceived: God cannot be mocked. A man reaps what he sows. The one who sows to please his sinful nature, from that nature will reap destruction; the one who sows to please the Spirit, from the Spirit will reap eternal life."   —Galatians 6:1-8 NIV

"'I am the vine; you are the branches. If a man remains in me and I in him, he will bear much fruit; apart from me you can do nothing. If anyone does not remain in me, he is like a branch that is thrown away and withers; such branches are picked up, thrown into the fire and burned.'"
                                                    —John 15:5-6 NIV

"You will say then, 'Branches were broken off so that I could be grafted in.' Granted. But they were broken off because of unbelief, and you stand by faith. Do not be arrogant, but be afraid. For if God did not spare the natural branches, he will not spare you either. Consider therefore the kindness and sternness of God:

sternness to those who fell, but kindness to you, provided that you continue in his kindness. Otherwise, you also will be cut off."

—Romans 11:19-22 NIV

"It is impossible for those who have once been enlightened, who have tasted the heavenly gift, who have shared in the Holy Spirit, who have tasted the goodness of the word of God and the powers of the coming age, if they fall away, to be brought back to repentance, because to their loss they are crucifying the Son of God all over again and subjecting him to public disgrace. . . . Even though we speak like this, dear friends, we are confident of better things in your case—things that accompany salvation."

—Hebrews 6:4-9 NIV

"For, uttering great swelling words of emptiness, they entice in the lusts of the flesh, by licentiousness, those who are indeed escaping from those who live in error; promising them liberty, while they themselves are bondservants of corruption; for a man is brought into bondage by whoever overcomes him. For if, after they have escaped the defilement of the world through the knowledge of the Lord and Savior Jesus Christ, they are again entangled in it and overcome, the last state has become worse for them than the first. For it would be better for them not to have known the way of righteousness, than, after knowing it, to turn back from the holy commandment delivered to them. But it has happened to them according to the true proverb, 'The dog turns to his own vomit again,' and 'the sow that has washed to wallowing in the mire.'"

—2 Peter 2:18-22

Do the above passages teach something contrary to the message of today's popular preachers? If so, then the reader will have to decide whom to believe—today's popular preachers, or the inspired Word of God.

Why believe the Bible?

Do your harbor doubts about the Bible? That should not be surprising, because this world in rebellion against God has surrounded us with attacks against the Bible. Public schools teach that life on earth came originated through a series of chemical accidents, without the need for a divine Creator. They teach that mankind came into existence because animals went through a long series of accidental mutations and survival of the fittest, contradicting the Bible's declaration that "God created man in his own image." (Gen. 1:27)

The public media surround us with explanations of this world, its history and current events, that completely ignore God and the Bible. Even many clergymen ridicule the Bible and dismiss it as a book filled with myths, fairy tales and contradictions—interesting poetic literature, but not to be taken seriously in much of what it says..

So, when considering the invitation to follow Jesus, you may find it necessary to examine the Bible to prove to yourself that it is what it claims to be, the inspired written Word of God.

I certainly had to make such an examination myself. As a teenager, I wanted to do things that appeared to be condemned by God and by the religion of my parents. So, it became convenient to stop believing in God. Moreover, I looked up to certain men and women of science who rejected any belief in God or the Bible. These great physicists and astronomers were my role models, and I wanted to grow up to pursue a career in their field. I read numerous books by atheistic scientists and philosophers, and soon became steeped in existentialist philosophy that left God and the Bible completely out of the picture. Some years later, when I matured a bit, I began to doubt whether a series of chemical accidents over millions of years could adequately explain the nobility, inner beauty and goodness that I saw in the best of mankind—or the even higher ideals that the best of humankind visualized as goals they reached for above and beyond themselves. Were those high ideals embodied in a God who created us and the world around us? Is the Bible really his inspired message to the human race? I began to seriously examine the evidence.

For those who are willing to examine it carefully and prayerfully, the evidence is overwhelming that the Bible is God's book of truth.

First of all, there is the honesty and candor of the Bible's historical account. In contrast to other ancient history books that typically glorified kings and emperors as almost godlike heroes without mentioning their flaws and human frailties, the Bible describes in detail, the strengths and the weaknesses of the kings of Israel, the ancient prophets, and the apostles of Christ. Even when telling about great king David, the Old Testament includes the sad episodes of his adulterous affair with Bathsheba and his fawning over rebellious Absalom.

King Solomon is presented as the wisest man who ever lived, but that wisdom did not prevent him from falling into idolatry when he broke God's laws by marrying foreign wives and began catering to their requests to worship false gods. And when the New Testament speaks of Jesus' apostles, it candidly tells of Judas's betrayal, Peter's weaknesses, Thomas's doubts, and an argument between Paul and Barnabas that prevented them from working together.

Unlike myths that are set 'once upon a time' in 'a land far away,' the history recorded in the Bible speaks of times, places and persons that are confirmed by contemporary secular histories and by modern archaeology. The Bible relates events in Israel and Judah to specific years in the reigns of Babylonian, Persian and Roman emperors known to secular historians. For example, Zechariah prophesied "In the eighth month, in the second year of Darius," the Medo-Persian emperor. (Zech. 1:1) It was due to a Roman census that Jesus' mother Mary traveled to Bethlehem and gave birth to him there, when "a decree went out from Caesar Augustus that all the world should be enrolled. This was the first enrollment made when Quirinius was governor of Syria." (Luke 2:1-2) John the Baptist began preaching "in the fifteenth year of the reign of Tiberius Caesar, Pontius Pilate being governor of Judea, and Herod being tetrarch of Galilee, and his brother Philip tetrarch of the region of Ituraea and Trachonitis, and Lysanias tetrarch of Abilene." (Luke 3:1)

Of course, honesty, candor and historical accuracy do not by themselves prove the Bible to be God's inspired Word. But prophecy does supply the additional needed proof. Men find it difficult to predict next week's weather. But the Bible contains so many predictions of future events that have come true with such consistent accuracy—even centuries later—that these fulfillments could not possibly have been due to chance. The One who inspired the writers of the Bible must have known and/or controlled the future—something only God could do.

The prophecies that prove the divine inspiration of the Scriptures fall into a number of categories.

Prophecies about the Messiah or Christ

The ancient Hebrew writers of the Old Testament wrote hundreds of years before Christ, but their writings include a number of prophecies that were fulfilled centuries later in the life and ministry of Jesus. "Beginning from Moses and from all the prophets, he explained to them in all the Scriptures the things concerning himself." (Luke 24:27)

For example, Micah 5:2 indicates that the promised Messiah would come from the town of Bethlehem in Judah, and this actually took place when Jesus was born in Bethlehem as recorded at Matthew 2:1-6 and Luke 2:4-7.

Psalm 22, written by king David roughly a thousand years before Christ, begins with words Jesus would speak on the cross (verse 1; compare Matt. 27:46 and Mark 15:34), goes on to describe how they would pierce his hands and his feet (verse 16), how enemies would ridicule him as he hung on the cross (verses 7-8; compare Matt. 27:41-43), and how they would cast lots and divide his clothing (verse 18; compare Matt. 27:35, Mark 15:24, Luke 23:34 and John 19:24).

Other prophecies that Jesus fulfilled centuries later include that he would be born of a virgin, that he would be a descendant of king David, that he would live in Nazareth, that he would preach in Galilee, that he would be betrayed for thirty pieces of silver, and that he would be buried in a rich man's tomb. There are actually dozens of Old Testament prophecies that were fulfilled in Christ. You will encounter them as you read the four Gospels. Or you can find them by searching the Internet.

Prophecies about the God of Abraham

There are prophecies throughout the Old Testament and the New Testament to the effect that the gods of the gentile nations—Baal, Ashtoreth, Chemosh, Dagon, Artemis, Zeus and the rest—would be abandoned and forgotten, while the God of Abraham would come to be worshiped worldwide by people of all nations.

Such predictions may have seemed laughable when they were made, because those other gods were much more popular than the unseen God of the tiny Hebrew nation, but today there are billions Christians, Jews and Muslims in all the nations of the world who profess to worship the God of Abraham.

The Bible's prophecies on this matter were written during an era when each nation had its own gods and goddesses. The Ammonites worshipped Molech, and sacrificed their children as part of that worship. The people of Phoenicia and Canaan bowed down to Baal and Ashtoreth. The nation of Moab served their god Chemosh. The Philistines prostrated themselves before Dagon. The Greeks in Ephesus shouted praise to their goddess Artemis. The Egyptians, Greeks and Romans worshipped their emperors and pharaohs as gods, along with a whole pantheon of pagan deities. But the people of Israel worshipped the unseen Creator of the universe, who revealed himself to Abraham and Abraham's offspring by the name Yahweh or Jehovah—the Hebrew tetragrammaton or word of four letters, YHWH (rendered in most modern English translations as LORD).

How many people today still worship Molech, Chemosh or Dagon? A better question might be, How many people today have even heard of these long-lost 'gods'? How many cities throughout the world can boast of temples where throngs of people assemble to pray to the Greek and Roman deities? But the God of Abraham has people who profess to worship him today in Jewish synagogues, in Catholic, Protestant and Orthodox churches and in Muslim mosques throughout the earth.

Did the God of Abraham win worshipers worldwide because the nations sponsoring other gods ceased to exist? At first glance, that might seem to be explain why Molech, Chemosh and Dagon find few faithful adherents today—the nations of Ammon, Phoenicia and Moab are no longer on the map. But, wait! Israel, too, ceased to exist as a nation some two thousand years ago, and wasn't re-established until very recently in 1948. Yet the God of Israel survived and gained worshipers throughout the earth. Moreover, Egypt still exists as a nation, but the gods of the pharaohs and the pyramids are long gone. The vast majority of Egyptians today profess to worship the God of Abraham. Greece and Rome are still on the map, but the Greeks worship the God of Abraham, and Rome has become synonymous with the Roman Catholic faith that elevates the God of Abraham and his Messiah or Christ.

Could it be a mere coincidence, then, that the God of Israel has worshipers everywhere, while the gods of Israel's ancient neighbors have faded into oblivion? No, this is exactly what the Bible prophesied would occur.

The Old Testament was written over a period of hundreds of years in the Hebrew language, and it was completed long before the third century B.C., when it was translated into Greek in Alexandria, Egypt. Contained within that Old Testament, while the pantheon of pagan gods were still actively worshiped, were these ancient prophecies about the God of Abraham:

"All the ends of the world shall remember and turn unto the LORD: and all the kindreds of the nations shall worship before thee." (Psalm 22:27 KJV)

"All the earth shall worship thee, and shall sing unto thee; they shall sing to thy name." (Psalm 66:4 KJV)

"That thy way may be known upon earth, thy saving health among all nations." (Psalm 67:2 KJV)

"God shall bless us; and all the ends of the earth shall fear him." (Psalm 67:7)

"All nations whom thou hast made shall come and worship before thee, O LORD; and shall glorify thy name." (Psalm 86:9 KJV)

"O LORD . . . the Gentiles shall come unto thee from the ends of the earth, and shall say, Surely our fathers have inherited lies, vanity, and things wherein there is no profit. Shall a man make gods unto himself, and they are no gods."(Jeremiah 16:19-20 KJV)

"And it shall come to pass, that every one that is left of all the nations which came against Jerusalem shall even go up from year to year to worship the King, the LORD of hosts." (Zechariah 14:16 KJV)

"'My name will be great among the nations, from the rising to the setting of the sun. In every place incense and pure offerings will be brought to my name, because my name will be great among the nations,' says the LORD Almighty." (Malachi 1:11 NIV)

How unlikely these words would have seemed to non-Israelites at the time when they were written, if non-Israelites would even have bothered to read the religious writings of the Jews!

Hundreds of years later the New Testament was completed and began circulating in multiple copies during the lifetime of those who encountered Jesus in the flesh—at a time when pagan Roman Caesars still ruled the world and compelled people to worship them as gods. Yet these early Christian writings, too, prophesy the same thing about the God of Abraham:

"Who shall not fear thee, O Lord, and glorify thy name? for thou only art holy: for all nations shall come and worship before thee; for thy judgments are made manifest." (Revelation 15:4 KJV)

How unlikely this, too, must have seemed at a time when the powerful Roman empire had only recently crushed Jewish nationalism, tore down the Jewish temple in Jerusalem, scattered the Jewish captives to the four corners of the empire, and was in the process of hunting down and publicly executing the remaining followers of the Jewish Messiah Jesus!

Yet, in spite of overwhelming odds, these ancient biblical prophecies have proved true. Paul, Barnabas and other early Christian disciples traveled far and wide, following Jesus' instructions to "go and make followers of all people in the world" (Matt. 28:19 NCV) and trusting Jesus' assurance that, "you will receive power when the Holy Spirit has come upon you; and you shall be My witnesses both in Jerusalem, and in all Judea and Samaria, and even to the remotest part of the earth." (Acts 1:8 NASB) Wherever they went among the Gentile nations 'ten men' would accept the message about the Jewish Messiah and would take up worshiping the God of the Bible, as foretold centuries earlier by the Hebrew prophet Zechariah: "Thus says Yahweh of Armies: 'In those days, ten men will take hold, out of all the languages of the nations, they will take hold of the skirt of him who is a Jew, saying, "We will go with you, for we have heard that God is with you."'" (Zechariah 8:23) And those who became believers went on to share the Bible's message with others, spreading the message of the God of the Bible far and wide.

The result is that today there are Christians in every land—along with Jews and Muslims who also profess to worship the God of Abraham. Yes, the God of Abraham is worshiped today by people in all the nations of the earth, just as prophesied in the Bible thousands of years ago. Against all odds, these ancient prophecies have come true—a stunning proof that the Bible is God's inspired Word.

Prophecies about Jerusalem, the Jewish people and Israel

As far back as the books of Moses written more than three thousand years ago, the Bible foretold that the Jewish people would be uprooted from the Promised Land and would be scattered throughout the world, hated by people everywhere, only to be restored as a nation thousands of years later, shortly before the end of the world. Impossible as it may have seemed, the Roman empire carried out that worldwide scattering and the British empire later facilitated the regathering.

Through Moses, God brought the nation of Israel into a covenant, a solemn agreement to keep the complete set of laws and commandments He gave them. "These are the words of the covenant which the LORD commanded Moses to make with the sons of Israel." (Deuteronomy 29:1 NASB) If they kept the covenant, they would receive a long string of blessings specifically listed as part of the agreement. But, if they broke the covenant, there would be punishments in store for the nation. The ultimate punishment would be the breakup of the nation and the scattering of the Jewish people to live as strangers in the territories of other nations.

"But it shall come about, if you do not obey the LORD your God . . . the LORD will scatter you among all peoples, from one end of the earth to the other end of the earth." (Deuteronomy 28:15, 64 NASB)

Though the Jewish people would remain in this scattered condition, without a homeland of their own, for a very long, long time, this scattering would not be permanent. They would eventually be returned to the Promised Land:

". . . then the LORD thy God will turn thy captivity, and have compassion upon thee, and will return and gather thee from all the nations, whither the LORD thy God hath scattered thee . . . from thence will he fetch thee: And the LORD thy God will bring thee into the land which thy fathers possessed, and thou shalt possess it." (Deuteronomy 30:3-5 KJV)

". . . the LORD will . . . assemble the dispersed of Israel, and gather together the scattered of Judah from the four corners of the earth." (Isaiah 11:11-12 Jewish Publication Society of America)

There were relatively brief periods of captivity forced on the Jews by the Assyrian empire and later by the Babylonian empire. Much of the population was carried captive to Babylon for about seventy years, with a large number of escapees fleeing in the other direction, to Egypt, around the sixth century B.C. But the real scattering of the Jews to the four corners of the earth was yet future. Jesus, the Jewish Messiah, repeated the prophecy in these words:

"'And they shall fall by the edge of the sword and be led away captive into all nations: and Jerusalem shall be trodden down of the Gentiles, until the times of the Gentiles be fulfilled.'" (Luke 21:24 KJV)

Within the lifetime of those who witnessed Christ's crucifixion, a Jewish uprising against Rome was crushed brutally by the imperial armies. The Romans demolished Jerusalem and its temple and sold the Jews into slavery throughout the empire, scattering them to the four corners of the earth, into all the nations.

Not only were the Jews scattered worldwide, but they were also hated worldwide—just at the Bible prophesied: "I will pursue them with the sword, famine and plague and will make them abhorrent to all the kingdoms of the earth and an object of cursing and horror, of scorn and reproach, among all the nations where I drive them." (Jer. 29:18 NIV) "You will be a hated thing to the nations where the LORD sends you: they will laugh at you and make fun of you." (Deut. 28:37 NCV) Pogroms and anti-Semitism followed the Jewish people wherever they went.

Normally, such worldwide scattering and persecution would have spelled the end of a people and a nation. To all appearances, there would never again be a Jewish state in Palestine. The Romans ruled the ruins of Jerusalem until the empire began to fall apart. Then the eastern empire ruled from Byzantium or Constantinople. With the rise of Islam, Muslims took control. Over the centuries the land changed hands as European Crusaders and the Arab warriors of Islamic Jihad pushed each other back and forth across the war-torn terrain. For hundreds of years—nearly two thousand years, in fact—Gentiles trampled upon Jerusalem. Would the Jewish state ever be restored? Only a miracle could bring that about.

However, that miracle had been promised in Bible prophecy. Although it took two world wars to accomplish it, the miracle occurred as the hand of God pushed world events in that direction, and the prophecy was fulfilled.

World War I was still raging, and the Ottoman Turks still held Jerusalem when, on June 4, 1917, Jules Cambon, Secretary General of the French Foreign Ministry, wrote this in an official letter to Jewish Zionist leader Nahum Sokolow: ". . . it would be a deed of justice and reparation to assist, by the protection of the Allied Powers, in the renaissance of the Jewish nationality in that Land from which the people of Israel were exiled so many centuries ago." Five months later, on November 2, 1917, British foreign secretary Arthur James Lord Balfour wrote in a letter to a Jewish peer in the House of Lords, an official pronouncement that has since been dubbed the Balfour Declaration: "His Majesty's Government view with favour the establishment in Palestine of a national home for the Jewish people . . ." These proclamations are reminiscent of the orders issued by rulers of the ancient Medo-Persian empire to rebuild Jerusalem and its temple after the Babylonian exile, as recorded in the Old Testament books of Nehemiah and Ezra.

When British forces under General Allenby took Jerusalem from the Ottoman Turks in December, 1917, a Jewish Legion of several thousand Jews from many nations formed part of the victorious army. Under a Mandate from the League of Nations, Britain administered the territory. Meanwhile, a steady influx of Jewish immigrants began to arrive.

As though to thwart the fulfillment of prophecy, Hitler's Nazi government arose and began the systematic slaughter of six million Jews in gas chambers and ovens. It took the Second World War to stop this demonic Holocaust and to keep the prophecy on track to fulfillment. But enough Jews survived to see the formation of the State of Israel in 1948. The Bible indeed proved to be a book of true prophecy.

These prophecies, undeniably fulfilled by events thousands of years after they were written, offer indisputable evidence of the truthfulness, inspiration and reliability of the Bible.

Unlike fanciful religious writings and fairy tales, the Bible speaks of the real world and its past and future events. The existence of ancient kings and kingdoms described in Scripture has been verified, time and again, by archaeological discoveries. In fact, archaeologists unearthing the history of the Middle East have long used the Bible as a guide, to help them know what to look for and where to dig for it. Besides its 'end times' prophecies concerning Messiah's return, his coming Kingdom of God, and the end of the corrupt 'world' as we know it, the Bible also contains many prophecies that have already undergone fulfillment. Their accurate fulfillment hundreds or thousands of years later offers convincing evidence to help us put faith in the Bible as the Word of God.

Who is Jesus?

If you are a Jew, you probably think of Jesus as the one Christians claim to be the Jewish Messiah, but whom Jews see as a pretender to that role. If you are a Muslim, you likely recognize Jesus as the one spoken of in the Islamic holy book, the Koran, as "Isa, son of Miriam." If you are non-religious, you no doubt recognize Jesus as the one whose birth was originally celebrated by the Christmas holiday, even though the holiday has since become centered around a fictitious Santa Claus, flying reindeer, and retail sales.

But, who is Jesus according to his original followers who spent years living with him and listening to his teachings?

"In the beginning was the Word, and the Word was with God, and the Word was God. The same was in the beginning with God. All things were made through him. Without him was not anything made that has been made.

"The Word became flesh, and lived among us. We saw his glory, such glory as of the one and only Son of the Father, full of grace and truth." —John 1:1-3, 14

The Apostle John, who wrote the above, was one of Jesus' earliest followers. He explains that Jesus is the eternal Son of God, who was with God the Father from the beginning. God sent his Son to save us from our sins and to give us eternal life:

"For God so loved the world, that he gave his one and only Son, that whoever believes in him should not perish, but have eternal life.

"For God didn't send his Son into the world to judge the world, but that the world should be saved through him." —John 3:16-17

Matthew and Luke—also early followers of Jesus—tell the story of how Jesus came into the world:

"The angel Gabriel was sent from God to a city of Galilee, named Nazareth, to a virgin . . .

"The angel said to her, 'Don't be afraid, Mary, for you have found favor with God. Behold, you will conceive in your womb, and bring forth a son, and will call his name "Jesus." He will be great, and will be called the Son of the Most High.'" —Luke 1:26-27, 30-32

"Now the birth of Jesus Christ was like this; for after his mother, Mary, was engaged to Joseph, before they came together, she was found pregnant by the Holy Spirit.

"Joseph, her husband, being a righteous man, and not willing to make her a public example, intended to put her away secretly. But when he thought about these things, behold, an angel of the Lord appeared to him in a dream, saying,

"'Joseph, son of David, don't be afraid to take to yourself Mary, your wife, for that which is conceived in her is of the Holy Spirit. She shall bring forth a son. You shall call his name Jesus, for it is he who shall save his people from their sins.'

"Now all this has happened, that it might be fulfilled which was spoken by the Lord through the prophet, saying, 'Behold, the virgin shall be with child, and shall bring forth a son. They shall call his name Immanuel; which is, being interpreted, "God with us."'

"Joseph arose from his sleep, and did as the angel of the Lord commanded him, and took his wife to himself; and didn't know her sexually until she had brought forth her firstborn son. He named him Jesus."   —Matthew 1:18-24

"A decree went out from Caesar Augustus that all the world should be enrolled. This was the first enrollment made when Quirinius was governor of Syria. All went to enroll themselves, everyone to his own city. Joseph also went up from Galilee, out of the city of Nazareth, into Judea, to the city of David, which is called Bethlehem, because he was of the house and family of David; to enroll himself with Mary, who was pledged to be married to him as wife, being pregnant. It happened, while they were there, that the day had come that she should give birth. She brought forth her firstborn son, and she wrapped him in bands of cloth, and laid him in a feeding trough, because there was no room for them in the inn. "There were shepherds in the same country staying in the field, and keeping watch by night over their flock. Behold, an angel of the Lord stood by them, and the glory of the Lord shone around them, and they were terrified.

"The angel said to them, 'Don't be afraid, for behold, I bring you good news of great joy which will be to all the people. For there is born to you, this day, in the city of David, a Savior, who is Christ the Lord.'"

—Luke 2:1-11

The familiar Christmas story, above, is not the whole story of Jesus, of course, but just the beginning. Peter, another very early follower, summarizes here Jesus' life and ministry—and the work Jesus assigned to his followers:

"Peter opened his mouth and said,

"'Truly I perceive that God doesn't show favoritism; but in every nation he who fears him and works righteousness is acceptable to him. The word which he sent to the children of Israel, preaching good news of peace by Jesus Christ—he is Lord of all—you yourselves know what happened, which was proclaimed throughout all Judea, beginning from Galilee, after the baptism which John preached; even Jesus of Nazareth, how God anointed him with the Holy Spirit and with power, who went about doing good and healing all who were oppressed by the devil, for God was with him.

"'We are witnesses of everything he did both in the country of the Jews, and in Jerusalem; whom they also killed, hanging him on a tree. God raised him up the third day, and gave him to be revealed, not to all the people, but to witnesses who were chosen before by God, to us, who ate and drank with him after he rose from the dead. He commanded us to preach to the people and to testify that this is he who is appointed by God as the Judge of the living and the dead. All the prophets testify about him, that through his name everyone who believes in him will receive remission of sins.'"

—Acts 10:34-43

Jesus' followers faithfully preached the message he taught them, and they trained others to do the same. Some of them wrote down the history of Jesus' life and ministry, resulting in the four Gospels of Matthew, Mark, Luke and John. These, together with letters to the early churches, make up the New Testament that we have today as part of God's inspired Word, the Bible.

The first part of the Bible, the Old Testament, tells the story of God's dealings with mankind before the birth of Christ, while the New Testament continues on from there.

This book quotes extensively from the Bible, but there is no substitute for reading the Bible itself. As you consider the invitation to "Come, follow Jesus!" you would do well to pick up the Bible itself and begin reading it—perhaps starting with Matthew at the beginning of the New Testament. This book highlights important Bible passages, and they should serve to whet your appetite for reading God's complete message to mankind, where you will learn much more about who Jesus is and how he can change your life. After all, he is not just an historical character in a book; rather, he is alive, and he is active in the lives of those who follow him. Jesus promises,

"'One who loves me will be loved by my Father, and I will love him, and will reveal myself to him.'" —John 14:21

Jesus reveals himself to us as our Savior who cares about each one of us personally and intimately:

"'My sheep listen to my voice; I know them, and they follow me. I give them eternal life, and they will never die, and no one can steal them out of my hand. My Father gave my sheep to me. He is greater than all, and no person can steal my sheep out of my Father's hand. The Father and I are one.'" —John 10:27-29 NCV

What did Jesus teach?

". . . Jesus began to preach, and to say, 'Repent! For the Kingdom of Heaven is at hand.'"
—Matthew 4:17

The word *repent* means to feel sorry for your past conduct, to regret or feel conscience-stricken about your past actions, attitudes, etc.—with such sorrow that you want to change your life for the better. Jesus began his ministry with a call for people to repent, and he also concluded his ministry by instructing his early followers to preach that same message:

"He told them, 'This is what is written: The Christ will suffer and rise from the dead on the third day, and repentance and forgiveness of sins will be preached in his name to all nations, beginning at Jerusalem.'"
—Luke 24:46-47 NIV

For people to repent from their sins means for them to be so sorry for their sins that they would quit practicing them and change their hearts and lives for the better. The call to "Repent!" was the opening theme of Jesus' teaching. It was also his closing theme—the message he assigned his followers to preach. So, this message of "repentance and forgiveness of sins" was the central theme of Jesus' preaching, the main point he wanted us to learn and to preach to others.

What else did Jesus teach? His other teaching all revolved around different aspects of repenting from our sins and receiving forgiveness for our sins. If we go through the four Gospels and analyze his words by topic, we find that Jesus devoted some of his teaching to salvation (about 4% of the words he spoke), the Kingdom of God (2%), the new covenant that he would institute (1%), and instructions for his followers to carry on their ministry (4%). But most of his words dealt with three major topics: discussing or proving by miracles his identity as the Messiah, the Son of God, the Savior who would save us from our sins (31%); outlining the behavior or conduct that God expects of us, so that we would be able to distinguish good behavior from sinful behavior (25%); and discussing rewards and punishments based on people's behavior or conduct (32%).

Jesus' words concerning rewards and punishments actually fall into three categories: punishment for that generation of Jews that sinned by rejecting Jesus (12%), and rewards and punishments people will receive after death (9%), or when Christ returns to judge this world (11%).

So, with 25% of Jesus' recorded words in the Gospels outlining the behavior God expects of us, and another 32% discussing rewards and punishments based on this conduct, that adds up to 57% of Jesus' message focusing on human behavior and its consequences, whether good or bad.

It is clear, then, that we have a lot to learn from reading Jesus' words, and that what we learn should affect the way we live our lives.

To see all of Jesus' teachings, please read the four Gospels of Matthew, Mark, Luke and John.   Meanwhile, here are a few sample excerpts to whet your appetite, so that you will go on to pick up the Bible and read the rest for yourself:

"'Blessed are those who hunger and thirst after righteousness, for they shall be filled. Blessed are the merciful, for they shall obtain mercy. Blessed are the pure in heart, for they shall see God. Blessed are the peacemakers, for they shall be called children of God. Blessed are those who have been persecuted for righteousness' sake, for theirs is the Kingdom of Heaven.

"'Blessed are you when people reproach you, persecute you, and say all kinds of evil against you falsely, for my sake. Rejoice, and be exceedingly glad, for great is your reward in heaven. For that is how they persecuted the prophets who were before you.'"

—Matthew 5:6-12

"'But woe to you who are rich! For you have received your consolation. Woe to you, you who are full now, for you will be hungry. Woe to you who laugh now, for you will mourn and weep. Woe, when men speak well of you, for their fathers did the same thing to the false prophets.'"   —Luke 6:24-26

"'But woe to you Pharisees! For you tithe mint and rue and every herb, but you bypass justice and the love of God. You ought to have done these, and not to have left the other un-done. Woe to you Pharisees! For you love the best seats in the synagogues, and the greetings in the market-places. Woe to you, scribes and Pharisees, hypocrites! For you are like hidden graves, and the men who walk over them don't know it.'

"One of the lawyers answered him, 'Teacher, in saying this you insult us also.'

"He said, 'Woe to you lawyers also! For you load men with burdens that are difficult to carry, and you yourselves won't even lift one finger to help carry those burdens.'"   —Luke 11:42-46

These excerpts from Jesus' teachings help us appreciate why many rich political and religious leaders, like the scribes and Pharisees, hated him and wanted to kill him.

"'You have heard that it was said, "An eye for an eye, and a tooth for a tooth." But I tell you, don't resist him who is evil; but whoever strikes you on your right cheek, turn to him the other also. If anyone sues you to take away your coat, let him have your cloak also. Whoever compels you to go one mile, go with him two. Give to him who asks you, and don't turn away him who desires to borrow from you.

"'You have heard that it was said, "You shall love your neighbor, and hate your enemy." But I tell you, love your enemies, bless those who curse you, do good to those who hate you, and pray for those who mistreat you and persecute you, that you may be children of your Father who is in heaven. For he makes his sun to rise on the evil and the good, and sends rain on the just and the unjust. For if you love those who love you, what reward do you have? . . .'"

—Matthew 5:38-46

"'Whenever you stand praying, forgive, if you have anything against anyone; so that your Father, who is in heaven, may also forgive you your transgressions. But if you do not forgive, neither will your Father in heaven forgive your transgressions.'"

—Mark 11:25-26

"Then Peter came and said to him, 'Lord, how often shall my brother sin against me, and I forgive him? Until seven times?'

"Jesus said to him, 'I don't tell you until seven times, but, until seventy times seven.

"'Therefore the Kingdom of Heaven is like a certain king, who wanted to reconcile accounts with his servants. When he had begun to reconcile, one was brought to him who owed him ten thousand talents. But because he couldn't pay, his lord commanded him to be sold, with his wife, his children, and all that he had, and payment to be made. The servant therefore fell down and kneeled before him, saying, "Lord, have patience with me, and I will repay you all!"

"'The lord of that servant, being moved with compassion, released him, and forgave him the debt.

"'But that servant went out, and found one of his fellow servants, who owed him one hundred denarii, and he grabbed him, and took him by the throat, saying, "Pay me what you owe!" So his fellow servant fell down at his feet and begged him, saying, "Have patience with me, and I will repay you!" He would not, but went and cast him into prison, until he should pay back that which was due. So when his fellow servants saw what was done, they were exceedingly sorry, and came and told to their lord all that was done. Then his lord called him in, and said to him, "You wicked servant! I forgave you all that debt, because you begged me. Shouldn't you also have had mercy on your fellow servant, even as I had mercy on you?" His lord was angry, and delivered him to the tormentors, until he should pay all that was due to him.

"'So my heavenly Father will also do to you, if you don't each forgive your brother from your hearts for his misdeeds.'"

—Matthew 18:21-35

These excerpts from Jesus' teachings also teach us the way we should live: being merciful and loving toward others, just as Jesus is merciful and loving toward us. (But his mercy and love do not excuse wickedness; Jesus condemned wicked conduct and called sinners to repent of their sins. So should we.)

"'Be careful that you don't do your charitable giving before men, to be seen by them, or else you have no reward from your Father who is in heaven. Therefore when you do merciful deeds, don't sound a trumpet before yourself, as the hypocrites do in the synagogues and in the streets, that they may get glory from men. Most certainly I tell you, they have received their reward. But when you do merciful deeds, don't let your left hand know what your right hand does, so that your merciful deeds may be in secret, then your Father who sees in secret will reward you openly.

"'When you pray, you shall not be as the hypocrites, for they love to stand and pray in the synagogues and in the corners of the streets, that they may be seen by men. Most certainly, I tell you, they have received their reward. But you, when you pray, enter into your inner room, and having shut your door, pray to your Father who is in secret, and your Father who sees in secret will reward you openly.'"

—Matthew 6:1-6

"'Don't lay up treasures for yourselves on the earth, where moth and rust consume, and where thieves break through and steal; but lay up for yourselves treasures in heaven, where neither moth nor rust consume, and where thieves don't break through and steal; for where your treasure is, there your heart will be also.'"

—Matthew 6:19-21

"He also said to the one who had invited him, 'When you make a dinner or a supper, don't call your friends, nor your brothers, nor your kinsmen, nor rich neighbors, or perhaps they might also return the favor, and pay you back. But when you make a feast, ask the poor, the maimed, the lame, or the blind; and you will be blessed, because they don't have the resources to repay you. For you will be repaid in the resurrection of the righteous.'"

—Luke 14:12-14

"'See the birds of the sky, that they don't sow, neither do they reap, nor gather into barns. Your heavenly Father feeds them. Aren't you of much more value than they?

"'Which of you, by being anxious, can add one moment to his life-span? Why are you anxious about clothing? Consider the lilies of the field, how they grow. They don't toil, neither do they spin, yet I tell you that even Solomon in all his glory was not dressed like one of these. But if God so clothes the grass of the field, which today exists, and tomorrow is thrown into the oven, won't he much more clothe you, you of little faith?

"'Therefore don't be anxious, saying, "What will we eat?", "What will we drink?" or, "With what will we be clothed?" For the Gentiles seek after all these things; for your heavenly Father knows that you need all these things. But seek first God's Kingdom, and his righteousness; and all these things will be given to you as well.

"'Therefore don't be anxious for tomorrow, for tomorrow will be anxious for itself. Each day's own evil is sufficient.'"

—Matthew 6:26-34

"They were bringing to him little children, that he should touch them, but the disciples rebuked those who were bringing them. But when Jesus saw it, he was moved with indignation, and said to them, 'Allow the little children to come to me! Don't forbid them, for the Kingdom of God belongs to such as these. Most certainly I tell you, whoever will not receive the Kingdom of God like a little child, he will in no way enter into it.' He took them in his arms, and blessed them, laying his hands on them."   —Mark 10:13-16

"'Again, the Kingdom of Heaven is like a dragnet, that was cast into the sea, and gathered some fish of every kind, which, when it was filled, they drew up on the beach. They sat down, and gathered the good into containers, but the bad they threw away. So will it be in the end of the world. The angels will come forth, and separate the wicked from among the righteous, and will cast them into the furnace of fire. There will be the weeping and the gnashing of teeth.'"   —Matthew 13:47-50

So, Jesus did not teach universal salvation (that *everyone* will be saved and enjoy rewards in heaven). Rather, wicked and disobedient people will face punishment after this life. This was a constant theme of Jesus' teaching, although it is not a popular message today. He makes this point very clear in the following passage:

"'But when the Son of Man comes in his glory, and all the holy angels with him, then he will sit on the throne of his glory. Before him all the nations will be gathered, and he will separate them one from another, as a shepherd separates the sheep from the goats. He will set the sheep on his right hand, but the goats on the left.

"'Then the King will tell those on his right hand, "Come, blessed of my Father, inherit the Kingdom prepared for you from the foundation of the world; for I was hungry, and you gave me food to eat. I was thirsty, and you gave me drink. I was a stranger, and you took me in. I was naked, and you clothed me. I was sick, and you visited me. I was in prison, and you came to me."

"'Then the righteous will answer him, saying, "Lord, when did we see you hungry, and feed you; or thirsty, and give you a drink? When did we see you as a stranger, and take you in; or naked, and clothe you? When did we see you sick, or in prison, and come to you?"

"'The King will answer them, "Most certainly I tell you, inasmuch as you did it to one of the least of these my brothers, you did it to me."

"'Then he will say also to those on the left hand, "Depart from me, you cursed, into the eternal fire which is prepared for the devil and his angels; for I was hungry, and you didn't give me food to eat; I was thirsty, and you gave me no drink; I was a stranger, and you didn't take me in; naked, and you didn't clothe me; sick, and in prison, and you didn't visit me."

"'Then they will also answer, saying, "Lord, when did we see you hungry, or thirsty, or a stranger, or naked, or sick, or in prison, and didn't help you?"

"'Then he will answer them, saying, "Most certainly I tell you, inasmuch as you didn't do it to one of the least of these, you didn't do it to me."

"'These will go away into eternal punishment, but the righteous into eternal life.'"
—Matthew 25:31-46

Jesus warned that his faithful followers would also be hated, just as he was hated, and that some would be killed. But he encouraged us to remain faithful and to trust in him. God's Spirit will carry us through our times of trial, and we will receive our reward in heaven with Jesus:

"'Behold, I send you out as sheep in the midst of wolves. Therefore be wise as serpents, and harmless as doves. But beware of men: for they will deliver you up to councils, and in their synagogues they will scourge you. Yes, and you will be brought before governors and kings for my sake, for a testimony to them and to the nations. But when they deliver you up, don't be anxious how or what you will say, for it will be given you in that hour what you will say. For it is not you who speak, but the Spirit of your Father who speaks in you.

"'Brother will deliver up brother to death, and the father his child. Children will rise up against parents, and cause them to be put to death. You will be hated by all men for my name's sake, but he who endures to the end will be saved.'"
—Matthew 10:16-22

"'Don't be afraid of those who kill the body, but are not able to kill the soul. Rather, fear him who is able to destroy both soul and body in Gehenna.

"'Aren't two sparrows sold for an assarion coin? Not one of them falls on the ground apart from your Father's will, but the very hairs of your head are all numbered. Therefore don't be afraid. You are of more value than many sparrows.

"'Everyone therefore who confesses me before men, him I will also confess before my Father who is in heaven. But whoever denies me before men, him I will also deny before my Father who is in heaven.'"
—Matthew 10:28-33

"'Do you think that I have come to give peace in the earth? I tell you, no, but rather division. For from now on, there will be five in one house divided, three against two, and two against three. They will be divided, father against son, and son against father; mother against daughter, and daughter against her mother; mother-in-law against her daughter-in-law, and daughter-in-law against her mother-in-law.'"
—Luke 12:51-53

"He called the multitude to himself with his disciples, and said to them, 'Whoever wants to come after me, let him deny himself, and take up his cross, and follow me. For whoever wants to save his life will lose it; and whoever will lose his life for my sake and the sake of the Good News will save it. For what does it profit a man, to gain the whole world, and forfeit his life? For what will a man give in exchange for his life? For whoever will be ashamed of me and of my words in this adulterous and sinful generation, the Son of Man also will be ashamed of him, when he comes in the glory of his Father with the holy angels.'"
—Mark 8:34-38

So, Jesus' teachings invite us to follow him, even at great personal cost to ourselves—perhaps even at the expense of our life. Following him involves trusting in him for salvation and adhering faithfully to the things Jesus taught.

"He said to them, 'Thus it is written, and thus it was necessary for the Christ to suffer and to rise from the dead the third day, and that repentance and remission of sins should be preached in his name to all the nations, beginning at Jerusalem.'" —Luke 24:46-47

True Christianity still preaches this same message today—the Gospel message that calls people to repent of their sins and receive forgiveness through Christ.

These few excerpts are only a sample of the things Jesus taught. You owe it to yourself and to God, to read the New Testament for yourself. In that way you will receive Jesus' teachings in their original context, and you will read how his first followers went on to explain those teachings. Read the Bible prayerfully—asking for insight, for understanding, for faith to believe, and for faith to act in obedience to Jesus and his teachings.

What is life really all about?

Would you start a business in an industry that you did not understand? Your venture would soon fail. Would start out in a new position of employment without knowing what your employer expected you to do? You would not be able to keep the job. In every human endeavor the people who succeed are those who understand what it is all about. And the same is true of life itself.

However, we start out our lives as infants, not knowing what life is all about. That doesn't matter at first, when we are very young, because our parents care for us and provide for all our needs. It is also their responsibility to teach us what life is all about. But what if they don't know, because their parents had failed to teach them, and their parents' parents had failed to teach them? Then we can't possibly find out what life is all about, unless we learn from another source.

In the real world, that is what actually happened. In the beginning God created the heavens and the earth, and created human beings. Our first parents, the first humans, had some insight into what life is all about because God dealt with them personally. But they rebelled against their Creator, and they gave birth to rebellious offspring.

". . . sin entered into the world through one man, and death through sin; and so death passed to all men, because all sinned."

—Romans 5:12

"One thing I have learned: God made people good, but they have found all kinds of ways to be bad."   —Ecclesiastes 7:29 NCV

As they continued to multiply and spread abroad to fill the earth, our ancestors drifted farther and farther away from God and failed to pass on to new generations any knowledge of what life is all about.

On a number of occasions God intervened in human affairs to remind us. Through the flood of Noah's day he wiped away a world that had become filled with violence and sin, and gave mankind a fresh start. But, as soon as enough generations had passed to build a sizeable population, they again forgot about God and rebelled against him. To stop them from building a technologically advanced society centered around a skyscraper they were building at Babel in the land now known as Iraq, God confused their languages—giving each family group its own speech and grammar, so that they could no longer work together. They were forced to give up their building project and move away from each other, eventually populating the far reaches of the earth.

As they spread abroad to remote places and lost contact with each other, the families of man did a poor job of passing on to their offspring any knowledge of the Creator and his purpose for human beings. Although most national groups retained some dim recollection of heavenly beings, and some even retained a story of the worldwide flood in their oral traditions, the stories became twisted through centuries of retelling by people who, themselves, were not faithful to God and who had no desire to live by his rules. Before long, people everywhere were bowing down to idols of wood, stone and metal, guided in their worship by priests and prophets who knew nothing of the true God.

Eventually God began to break this cycle of ignorance by speaking to a man named Abram, whom he renamed Abraham. God later revealed himself to Abraham's son Isaac and to Isaac's son Jacob, whom God renamed Israel. Many generations later, when Israel's offspring had multiplied greatly and found themselves enslaved in Egypt, God sent Moses to free them from bondage and to bring them into a covenant or agreement with God.

Each party to the covenant made promises. God promised to give the Israelites the land of Canaan (whose inhabitants he had sentenced to death for their gross sins), and to bless the Israelites there as a special nation living under his laws. And, as their part of the agreement, the Israelites were obligated to obey God's laws, which included not worshiping any false gods. But the covenant also contained a clause spelling out what would happen if they broke the agreement: God would uproot them from the Promised Land and would scatter them worldwide among other nations that would hate and abuse them.

As far as the Jewish people were concerned, based on what God had revealed up to that time in history, life was all about keeping the laws God had given to them. Moses told them

"The secret things belong to the LORD our God, but the things revealed belong to us and to our children forever, that we may follow all the words of this law." —Deuteronomy 29:29 NIV

Wise king Solomon investigated the alternative pursuits that people came up with on their own, trying to give some other meaning to their lives, and he concluded that all of these pursuits were "vanity and a chasing after wind" (Eccl. 1:14; 2:11, 17, 26; 4:16; 6:9) Rather, he reached this inspired conclusion as to the real meaning of life:

"This is the end of the matter. All has been heard. Fear God, and keep his commandments; for this is the whole duty of man. For God will bring every work into judgment, with every hidden thing, whether it is good, or whether it is evil." —Ecclesiastes 12:13-14

Most of the Old Testament consists of the historical record detailing how the Israelites repeatedly broke their covenant with God and took up the worship of false gods, and how the true God punished them repeatedly to discipline them. Eventually, he announced to them that he would institute a new covenant that would be superior to the covenant they had broken. The new covenant would include forgiveness of sins, a closer personal relationship with God, and opportunity for non-Israelites—people from all nations—to know and worship the true God. Those who enter the new covenant receive a fuller understanding of what life is all about.

The New Testament introduces this new covenant and tells how people of many varied nationalities quit worshiping their idols and entered into this new covenant mediated through Jesus. For example, the Apostle Paul said this to an audience of pagan idol worshipers in ancient Athens, Greece:

". . . we ought not to think that the Divine Nature is like gold, or silver, or stone, engraved by art and design of man. The times of ignorance therefore God overlooked. But now he commands that all people everywhere should repent, because he has appointed a day in which he will judge the world in righteousness by the man whom he has ordained; of which he has given assurance to all men, in that he has raised him from the dead." —Acts 17:29-31

Many pagans in Paul's audience there in Athens and in other cities he visited around the Mediterranean Sea left behind the worship of false deities and embraced Christianity, coming under the new covenant mediated by Jesus. When we turn to "Jesus the mediator of the new covenant" (Heb. 12:24 KJV) we are adopted as God's children and we receive the Holy Spirit as Jesus promised. The eighth chapter of Paul's letter to the Roman congregation discusses this at some length.

"There is therefore now no condemnation to those who are in Christ Jesus, who don't walk according to the flesh, but according to the Spirit. . . . Those who are in the flesh can't please God. But you are not in the flesh but in the Spirit, if it is so that the Spirit of God dwells in you.

"But if any man doesn't have the Spirit of Christ, he is not his. If Christ is in you . . . if the Spirit of him who raised up Jesus from the dead dwells in you, he who raised up Christ Jesus from the dead will also give life to your mortal bodies through his Spirit who dwells in you. . . .

"For as many as are led by the Spirit of God, these are children of God. For you didn't receive the spirit of bondage again to fear, but you received the Spirit of adoption, by whom we cry, 'Abba! Father!' The Spirit himself testifies with our spirit that we are children of God; and if children, then heirs; heirs of God, and joint heirs with Christ; if indeed we suffer with him, that we may also be glorified with him.

"For I consider that the sufferings of this present time are not worthy to be compared with the glory which will be revealed toward us."
—Romans 8:1-18

This closer relationship with God—through our adoption as his children and our receiving his Holy Spirit—gives us greater appreciation of the meaning of life. And this relationship is not one that ends tragically in death, but rather an everlasting relationship that will only grow as time goes on, with a glorious future. Knowing that this is what life is really all about helps us put our present sufferings into a larger perspective. Momentary suffering today becomes insignificant when we compare it to what lies ahead for us. And the love of God revealed to us through Jesus strengthens us to face any sort of trouble in this world. As Paul wrote:

"Who shall separate us from the love of Christ? Could oppression, or anguish, or persecution, or famine, or nakedness, or peril, or sword? Even as it is written, 'For your sake we are killed all day long. We were accounted as sheep for the slaughter.' No, in all these things, we are more than conquerors through him who loved us.

"For I am persuaded, that neither death, nor life, nor angels, nor principalities, nor things present, nor things to come, nor powers, nor height, nor depth, nor any other created thing, will be able to separate us from the love of God, which is in Christ Jesus our Lord.
—Romans 8:35-39

Jesus came in the flesh so that he could set the example by suffering for us on the cross, so that we might be adopted as children of God:

"Since the children have flesh and blood, he too shared in their humanity so that by his death he might destroy him who holds the power of death—that is, the devil—and free those who all their lives were held in slavery by their fear of death."— Hebrews 2:14-15 NIV

The devil can no longer use our fear of death to force us to do evil, because we have been adopted as God's children with the hope of a glorious future forever in heaven. Christ, the captain of our salvation, suffered for us, to set us free from slavery to this sinful world.

"For it was fitting for Him, for whom are all things and by whom are all things, in bringing many sons to glory, to make the captain of their salvation perfect through sufferings."
—Hebrews 2:10 NKJV

God's purpose is to bring many sons to glory—to adopt us as his children and bring us to heaven to live with him in glory. We can't really understand the meaning of life without grasping this.

This "mystery," or "secret" as some translations put it, was kept from mankind over the centuries until God revealed it through the New Testament. The Apostle Paul referred to it as

"the mystery that has been kept hidden for ages and generations, but is now disclosed to the saints. To them God has chosen to make known among the Gentiles the glorious riches of this mystery, which is Christ in you, the hope of glory."

—Colossians 1:26-27 NIV

God is ready to destroy this wicked world in rebellion against him, but he holds back that destructive power at this time, while he continues to prepare us for the glorious eternal life to come:

"What if God, willing to show his wrath, and to make his power known, endured with much patience vessels of wrath made for destruction, and that he might make known the riches of his glory on vessels of mercy, which he prepared beforehand for glory, us, whom he also called, not from the Jews only, but also from the Gentiles?" —Romans 9:22-24

If we understand that our present circumstances in this world are only temporary, and that eternal glory awaits us, this can give us the strength and courage to endure the troubles we face now:

"Therefore we do not lose heart. Though outwardly we are wasting away, yet inwardly we are being renewed day by day. For our light and momentary troubles are achieving for us an eternal glory that far outweighs them all. So we fix our eyes not on what is seen, but on what is unseen. For what is seen is temporary, but what is unseen is eternal." —2 Corinthians 4:16-18 NIV

In just a short time—short compared to the eternity of joy ahead of us—Jesus will return to take us home with him. Or, if we die before his return, he will raise us to life:

"Behold, I tell you a mystery. We will not all sleep, but we will all be changed, in a moment, in the twinkling of an eye, at the last trumpet. For the trumpet will sound, and the dead will be raised incorruptible, and we will be changed. For this corruptible must put on incorruption, and this mortal must put on immortality. But when this corruptible will have put on incorruption, and this mortal will have put on immortality, then what is written will happen: 'Death is swallowed up in victory.' 'Death, where is your sting? Hades, where is your victory?'

"The sting of death is sin, and the power of sin is the law. But thanks be to God, who gives us the victory through our Lord Jesus Christ. Therefore, my beloved brothers, be steadfast, immovable, always abounding in the Lord's work, because you know that your labor is not in vain in the Lord."   —1 Corinthians 15:51-58

So, although king Solomon declared all human endeavors to be "vanity and a chasing after wind" (Eccl. 1:14; 2:11, 17, 26; 4:16; 6:9), our labor is not in vain in the Lord. He gives us the victory over death, and wipes every tear from our eyes. The meaning of life becomes clear when we have eternity in view.

"Therefore they are before the throne of God, they serve him day and night in his temple. He who sits on the throne will spread his tabernacle over them. They will never be hungry, neither thirsty any more; neither will the sun beat on them, nor any heat; for the Lamb who is in the midst of the throne shepherds them, and leads them to springs of waters of life. And God will wipe away every tear from their eyes."   —Revelation 7:15-17

Angels and demons

Besides the physical world that we can all see and that scientists can measure and investigate, there is also a hidden world that we can learn about only through divine revelation—or when beings from that world interact openly with this world. That hidden world is populated with spirit sons of God.

The Bible says relatively little about these spirit sons of God, although it includes mention of them from Genesis through Revelation, and what it does reveal is of critical importance to our understanding of the world we live in.

We know that angels existed before the creation of the earth, because "all the sons of God shouted for joy" when God "laid the foundations of the earth." (Job 38:4-7) God then created man "a little lower than the angels." (Heb. 2:7) A vision of God's throne in heaven shows that there are vast numbers of angels: "angels around the throne . . . the number of them was ten thousands of ten thousands, and thousands of thousands." (Rev. 5:11)

The Bible speaks of different types or categories of angels: holy angels including cherubs and seraphs—and fallen angels or demons. Holy angels serve God in the invisible realm and visit humans on rare occasions as messengers from God or to execute his judgments. For example, when the first humans sinned and were expelled from the garden of Eden, angels were posted to keep them from returning there. (Gen. 3:24) And Jesus' birth was announced to shepherds near Bethlehem by an angel. (Luke 2:8-14)

Only two holy angels are actually mentioned by name in the Bible: Gabriel who is named by Daniel and Luke, and Michael who is named in the books of Daniel, Jude and Revelation.

When they do visit humans, holy angels make it clear that they are humble messengers doing God's bidding, not their own, and they do not accept worship or otherwise interact inappropriately with humans. For example, when the Apostle John was shown visions by an angel, he said

"I fell down to worship at the feet of the angel who had been showing them to me. But he said to me, 'Do not do it! I am a fellow servant with you and with your brothers the prophets and of all who keep the words of this book. Worship God!'"

—Revelation 22:8-9 NIV

Fallen angels, on the other hand, seek or demand worship. When Satan the devil tempted Jesus in the wilderness, he wanted Jesus to worship him:

"Again, the devil took him to an exceedingly high mountain, and showed him all the kingdoms of the world, and their glory. He

said to him, 'I will give you all of these things, if you will fall down and worship me.'" —Matthew 4:8-9

And the Apostle Paul indicated that the worship of pagan idolaters is directed toward demons rather than toward God:

"What am I saying then? That a thing sacrificed to idols is anything, or that an idol is anything? But I say that the things which the Gentiles sacrifice, they sacrifice to demons, and not to God, and I don't desire that you would have fellowship with demons." —1 Corinthians 10:19-20

Just as "God made people good, but they have found all kinds of ways to be bad" (Eccl. 7:29 NCV), the fallen angels too appear to have exercised their free will to rebel against God. The first one to do so evidently became their chief or leader—like an organized crime boss in the visible world. Scripture calls him the devil (from a Greek word meaning *slanderer*) or Satan (from a Hebrew word meaning *adversary*). A parable directed at the king of Tyre seems to indicate that he was the cherub assigned to care for things on earth when the first humans were placed in the garden of Eden:

"You were in Eden, the garden of God . . . You were the anointed cherub who covers . . . You were perfect in your ways from the day that you were created, until unrighteousness was found in you. . . . you have sinned: therefore I have cast you as profane out of the mountain of God; and I have destroyed you, covering cherub, from the midst of the stones of fire. Your heart was lifted up because of your beauty; you have corrupted your wisdom by reason of your brightness . . ." —Ezekiel 28:13-17

A comparison of Genesis and Revelation also indicates that Satan the devil was the one who spoke through the serpent that deceived the first woman Eve:

"Now the serpent was more subtle than any animal of the field which Yahweh God had made. He said to the woman, 'Has God really said, "You shall not eat of any tree of the garden?"'"

"The woman said to the serpent, 'Of the fruit of the trees of the garden we may eat, but of the fruit of the tree which is in the middle of the garden, God has said, "You shall not eat of it, neither shall you touch it, lest you die."'"

"The serpent said to the woman, 'You won't surely die, for God knows that in the day you eat it, your eyes will be opened, and you will be like God, knowing good and evil.'" —Genesis 3:1-5

According to the Revelation recorded by the Apostle John, the serpent that deceived Eve was actually Satan the devil:

"the old serpent, he who is called the devil and Satan, the deceiver of the whole world" —Revelation 12:9

By lying to the woman and leading Adam and Eve to sin, punishable by death, Satan showed himself to be a liar and a murderer. Jesus said,

". . . the devil . . . He was a murderer from the beginning, not holding to the truth, for there is no truth in him. When he lies, he speaks his native language, for he is a liar and the father of lies."

—John 8:44 NIV

We cannot speak with certainty about matters that the Bible only hints at with vague references, but there are enough clues in Scripture to conclude that the cherub who was left in charge of matters on earth, and who abused his privileges, still retains control—somewhat like a human president who has been impeached for misconduct and abuse of power but has not yet been removed from office. When Satan tempted Jesus in the wilderness, he offered him worldly political power:

"The devil, leading him up on a high mountain, showed him all the kingdoms of the world in a moment of time. The devil said to him, 'I will give you all this authority, and their glory, for it has been delivered to me; and I give it to whomever I want. If you therefore will worship before me, it will all be yours.'" —Luke 4:5-7

Jesus did not dispute Satan's claim to world rulership with the ability to give political power to others, but instead answered

"'It is written: "Worship the Lord your God and serve him only."'"
—Luke 4:8 NIV

Later, Jesus referred to the devil as "the prince of this world" (John 14:30) or "the ruler of this world." (John 14:30 RSV, NKJV, NASB) And elsewhere Jesus said, "Now is the time for the world to be judged; now the ruler of this world will be thrown down." (John 12:31 NCV)

God's judgment may seem to us humans to be a long time in coming, but that is just because we are looking at things from a human perspective. From God's eternal perspective, and from the perspective of angels who were alive when the earth was created, the legal case against Satan is moving right along:

"But don't forget this one thing, beloved, that one day is with the Lord as a thousand years, and a thousand years as one day. The Lord is not slow concerning his promise, as some count slowness; but is patient with us, not wishing that any should perish, but that all should come to repentance. But the day of the Lord will come as a thief in the night . . ." —2 Peter 3:8-10

These disobedient angels face a time of judgment from God, according to the Apostle Peter who wrote that

". . . God didn't spare angels when they sinned, but cast them down to Tartarus, and committed them to pits of darkness, to be reserved for judgment" —2 Peter 2:4

But, in the meantime, they continue to deceive and tempt humans, evidently trying to justify themselves by pointing out the sins of others. Note the case of Job, where the curtain was pulled back so that we could see what went on in heaven before tragedy struck the family of this godly man:

"One day the angels came to present themselves before the LORD, and Satan also came with them.

"The LORD said to Satan, 'Where have you come from?'

"Satan answered the LORD, 'From roaming throughout the earth, going back and forth on it.'

"Then the LORD said to Satan, 'Have you considered my servant Job? There is no one on earth like him; he is blameless and upright, a man who fears God and shuns evil.'

"'Does Job fear God for nothing?' Satan replied, 'Have you not put a hedge around him and his household and everything he has? You have blessed the work of his hands, so that his flocks and herds are spread throughout the land. But now stretch out your hand and strike everything he has, and he will surely curse you to your face.'

"The LORD said to Satan, 'Very well, then, everything he has is in your power, but on the man himself do not lay a finger.'

"Then Satan went out from the presence of the LORD.'"

—Job 1:6-12 NIV

Satan went off from that meeting and sent fire, enemy raiders and a wind storm against Job's property and his family, destroying his possessions and killing all of his children. In spite of all this, Job kept his integrity. So, Satan took the matter further:

"Then the LORD said to Satan, 'Have you considered my servant Job? There is no one on earth like him; he is blameless and upright, a man who fears God and shuns evil. And he still maintains his integrity, though you incited me against him to ruin him without any reason.'

"'Skin for skin!' Satan replied. 'A man will give all he has for his own life. But now stretch out your hand and strike his flesh and bones, and he will surely curse you to your face.'

"The LORD said to Satan, 'Very well, then, he is in your hands; but you must spare his life.'

"So Satan went out from the presence of the LORD and afflicted Job with painful sores from the soles of his feet to the crown of his head. Then Job took a piece of broken pottery and scraped himself with it as he sat among the ashes.

"His wife said to him, 'Are you still maintaining your integrity? Curse God and die!'

"He replied, 'You are talking like a foolish woman. Shall we accept good from God, and not trouble?'

"In all this, Job did not sin in what he said."   —Job 2:3-10 NIV

Was Job's case unique? Or, is the devil still involved in making similar challenges regarding Christians today? Evidently the latter is the case, because the book of Revelation calls him

"the devil and Satan, the deceiver of the whole world. . . . '. . . the accuser of our brothers . . . who accuses them before our God day and night.'"   —Revelation 12:9-10

The Apostle Paul encouraged Christians in the ancient city of Ephesus to trust in Christ's strength and rely upon God because we have a struggle against powerful invisible enemies—the devil and his demons:

"Finally, be strong in the Lord, and in the strength of his might. Put on the whole armor of God, that you may be able to stand against the wiles of the devil. For our wrestling is not against flesh and blood, but against the principalities, against the powers, against the world's rulers of the darkness of this age, and against the spiritual forces of wickedness in the heavenly places."

—Ephesians 6:10-12

What does "the whole armor of God" consist of? Paul elaborates by listing these elements of our Christian walk as followers of Jesus: truth, righteousness, the Good News or Gospel message, faith, salvation, the Scriptures and prayer:

"Therefore put on the whole armor of God, that you may be able to withstand in the evil day, and, having done all, to stand. Stand therefore, having the utility belt of truth buckled around your waist, and having put on the breastplate of righteousness, and having fitted your feet with the preparation of the Good News of peace; above all, taking up the shield of faith, with which you will be able to quench all the fiery darts of the evil one. And take the helmet of salvation, and the sword of the Spirit, which is the word of God; with all prayer and requests, praying at all times in the Spirit, and being watchful to this end in all perseverance and requests for all the saints . . ."   —Ephesians 6:13-18

So, even though the devil and his demons are powerful invisible enemies, we can successfully stand firm against them if we put on "the whole armor of God" as Paul outlines here.

The Apostle Peter likewise encourages us to take our stand against the devil, trusting that God will bring us through our present sufferings in this world:

"Be sober and self-controlled. Be watchful. Your adversary, the devil, walks around like a roaring lion, seeking whom he may devour. Withstand him steadfast in your faith, knowing that your brothers who are in the world are undergoing the same sufferings. But may the God of all grace, who called you to his eternal glory by Christ Jesus, after you have suffered a little while, perfect, establish, strengthen, and settle you."   —1 Peter 5:8-10

While some of Satan's attacks against Christians are head-on violent confrontations, as in the case of Job, we must also be watchful for his more subtle attacks. Satan pretends to be a good angel, and humans who work for him similarly may appear on the outside to be good people. These more subtle attacks often occur inside Christian churches where false teachers employed by the devil do his bidding and attempt to lead church members and newcomers away from following Jesus:

"For such men are false apostles, deceitful workers, masquerading as Christ's apostles. And no wonder, for even Satan masquerades as an angel of light. It is no great thing therefore if his servants also masquerade as servants of righteousness, whose end will be according to their works."   —2 Corinthians 11:13-15

Such subtle attacks within Christian churches by "Christian" leaders who actually work for the devil are discussed in greater detail elsewhere in this book, particularly in the chapters that deal with Jezebel in the churches, and religious authorities, and those who deliberately keep on sinning.

God is temporarily tolerating the rebellion by Satan and his hordes of fallen angels, just as he is temporarily tolerating human rebellion and the wicked society men have built in the visible world around us. But the legal and moral issues raised by those who challenge God have been settled. The mountain of evidence that has piled up over the course of history proves that God is fully justified in executing judgment against rebellious angels and humans. Jesus indicated that their end will be in

"the eternal fire which is prepared for the devil and his angels"

—Matthew 25:41

Meanwhile, Satan's biggest 'success' has involved convincing the modern world that he does not exist. Not only does this allow him more easily to deceive and mislead people, but it also allows him to call into question the Bible's truthfulness, since it speaks of the devil from beginning to end. Those who call themselves Christians but do not believe the devil exists end up following a different Jesus—not the Jesus of the Bible who was tempted by the devil, who warned his followers against the devil, and whose purpose in coming was "to destroy the devil's work" as Jesus' beloved Apostle John points out here:

"Dear children, do not let anyone lead you the wrong way. Christ is righteous. So to be like Christ a person must do what is right. The devil has been sinning since the beginning, so anyone who continues to sin belongs to the devil. The Son of God came for this purpose: to destroy the devil's work.

"Those who are God's children do not continue sinning, because the new life from God remains in them. They are not able to go on sinning, because they have become children of God. So we can see who God's children are and who the devil's children are: Those who do not do what is right are not God's children, and those who do not love their brothers and sisters are not God's children."

—1 John 3:7-10 NCV

Jesus destroyed the devil's work through his sacrificial death on the cross:

"Since the children have flesh and blood, he too shared in their humanity so that by his death he might destroy him who holds the power of death—that is, the devil—and free those who all their lives were held in slavery by their fear of death."— Hebrews 2:14-15 NIV

The devil brought death to humankind, and enslaved us to sin through our fear of death. But Jesus lived a sinless life and died on the cross to set us free from both sin and death—setting us free from the power of the devil.

Gray areas, mysteries and religious authorities

When you first accept the invitation to come follow Jesus, it is a joyful time and it is a simple matter of trusting him to save you from your sins, obeying him as your new Lord, and looking for his promised return while fellowshipping with his people. But as you continue to interact with others in the churches, you will begin to encounter some of the issues and questions that have divided professed Christians over the centuries.

To what extent do we humans exercise free will, and to what extent are our actions and final destiny foreknown or even pre-determined by God? You will encounter pastors, teachers and theologians who say that it is all up to us—our free choice when we exercise our free will—and they will list numerous Bible verses to prove their point. But you will encounter other pastors, teachers and theologians who say it is all up to God—that all of these matters have been predetermined for us by God's sovereign will—and they will list numerous other Bible verses to prove their point. Who is correct? Or could both sides be missing the point?

Exactly how will events unfold in fulfillment of the prophecies about Christ's return? There are many schools of thought—dispensationalists, futurists, historicists, full preterists, partial preterists, and so on—each with an array of arguments to present supported by selected Bible verses with their own preferred interpretations. Which of them are right? Or, will the actual unfolding of events surprise them all?

What does the Bible say about birth control, motion pictures, masturbation, blood transfusions, drinking coffee or tea, and driving automobiles? It says nothing at all—not one word for or against any of these. Yet you will find religious authorities who issue rules on all of these matters as if they were speaking for God, and who will point to passages in the Bible as justification for their strongly worded proclamations or prohibitions.

As a result, these questions concerning prophecy, free will and human behavior help form the dividing lines between some of the various Christian churches and denominations.

What is the problem? Is it that the Bible is ambiguous, confusing and open to every sort of interpretation on all sorts of matters? No, not at all. The Bible is very clear and unambiguous on most of the matters that it discusses. But there are certain matters that it does not discuss at all. And there are certain other areas where God intentionally inspired the writers of the Bible to leave the answers unclear.

Consider, for example, how Jesus answered his Apostles when they met with him after his resurrection from the dead. They wanted to know when the remaining prophecies about the Messiah would be fulfilled, but notice the answer Jesus gave them:

"Therefore when they had come together, they asked him, 'Lord, are you now restoring the kingdom to Israel?' He said to them, 'It isn't for you to know times or seasons which the Father has set within his own authority. But you will receive power when the Holy Spirit has come upon you. You will be witnesses to me in Jerusalem, in all Judea and Samaria, and to the uttermost parts of the earth.'" —Acts 1:6-7

Jesus told them "it isn't for you to know" the answer to that question, but he did tell them what they were to do in the meantime. Essentially, he told them to 'mind their own business' and made clear what their business was—the witnessing work he assigned them to do.

Something similar was said centuries earlier to the Israelites when they were about to enter the Promised Land after being freed from captivity in Egypt. Through Moses, God had given them hundreds of laws to guide them in their worship and in their daily activities. But there were other matters that God did not reveal to them. So, Moses told them

"The secret things belong to the LORD our God, but the things revealed belong to us and to our children forever, that we may follow all the words of this law." —Deuteronomy 29:29 NIV

So, there were some things that God had revealed—written in the Law of Moses—and Moses told the nation of Israel that it was their responsibility to follow and obey those things. But there were other things that God kept secret, and those things belonged to God. As far as the people of Israel were concerned, those things were none of their business. Moses told them, essentially to mind their own business—leave the secret things to God, and be concerned with obeying the laws he gave them.

We today are not under the Law of Moses—we are under the Law of Christ—but the same principle applies. There are things God has told us, and it is our responsibility to obey. But there are other questions that we might want to ask, and to some of those questions God's answer is, essentially, 'Mind your own business!' As Moses told the Israelites, the secret things belong to God, but our job is to obey the Law of Christ that is stated clearly in the Bible.

We are reminded of this in one of my favorite Christian hymns titled "Trust and Obey." The chorus says, "Trust and obey, For there's no other way, To be happy in Jesus, But to trust and obey."

The Apostle Paul pointed out that there are things we won't understand or see clearly until we join Jesus in heaven

"For now we see through a glass, darkly; but then face to face: now I know in part; but then shall I know even as also I am known."

—1 Corinthians 13:12 KJV

Or, as the New International Version puts the same verse,

"Now we see but a poor reflection as in a mirror; then we shall see face to face. Now I know in part; then I shall know fully, even as I am fully known." —1 Corinthians 13:12 NIV

An ancient metal mirror or looking-glass might have offered a fuzzy or blurred reflection of the things viewed through it, rather than a sharp and clear image. And that is how it is with our understanding of God and his secret things. We won't see clearly until we reach his presence in heaven.

This principle is important to keep in mind when we worry about our loved ones, or people who never heard about Christ. Is God going to punish them unfairly? Sometimes people get their theology from Dante's Inferno or from popular Christian books, and they think God will be unfair. These writers, of course, can't possibly know anything more than what you and I know when we read the Bible, but they often expound in detail on matters that the Bible leaves ambiguous or unclear. Ordinary believers read their writings, and then they worry about whether God will be fair when he judges certain people.

This is where trust comes in. The things that are secret belong to God, and we need to trust him in these areas. Abraham worried when he heard that God was going to destroy Sodom and Gomorrah for their sins After all, he had relatives living there: his nephew Lot, and Lot's family:

Abraham approached God and asked,

"'Will you sweep away the righteous with the wicked? What if there are fifty righteous people in the city? Will you really sweep it away and not spare the place for the sake of the fifty righteous people in it? Far be it from you to do such a thing—to kill the righteous with the wicked, treating the righteous and the wicked alike. Far be it from you! Will not the Judge of all the earth do right?'"

—Genesis 18:23-25 NIV

Of course God will do the right thing. He discussed the matter back and forth with Abraham, and assured him he would not destroy the place even if only ten righteous people were found there. As it turned out, God removed to safety Abraham's nephew Lot, along with Lot's wife and two daughters, before raining destruction from the sky.

Usually we don't have the opportunity to engage in a back and forth conversation with God the way Abraham did in this case, receiving very clear answers to our questions. Then it becomes a matter of trust. Isn't Jesus our model of love and fairness and goodness? Doesn't he care about people even more than we do—enough to suffer and die on the cross for others? Won't he do what is right? Yes, we have every reason to trust him to do the good thing, the right and loving thing, when it comes to caring for others. If some writer or teacher has told you that Jesus will do something that does not seem right or fair, why believe such an authority? Instead, believe Jesus himself. Believe what you read in the Bible itself, rather than someone else's interpretation of the Bible.

Unfortunately, there are many teachers and preachers and religious 'authorities' who are all too happy to fill in the Bible's ambiguities and gray areas with their own dogmatic statements. Really, though, they have no sound basis for assertions beyond what any ordinary person could learn from reading the Bible itself. They would do well to listen to the Apostle Paul's counsel

"not to go beyond what is written, that none of you may be puffed up in favor of one against another." —1 Corinthians 4:6 RSV

What Jesus revealed about life after death

Although there are theologians and religious authorities who write or speak at great length about life after death, the Bible actually has comparatively little to say on the subject. And what it does say is rather sketchy and incomplete. This is not because God forgot to include more detail when he inspired the Bible writers. Rather, it is intentional on God's part. He gives us what we need to know, so that we can do what is right, but does not satisfy our curiosity with unnecessary details. As Moses told the Israelites,

"The secret things belong to the LORD our God, but the things revealed belong to us and to our children forever, that we may follow all the words of this law." —Deuteronomy 29:29 NIV

God gave the writers of the Old Testament only the barest of hints about life after death.

Job knew that he would be redeemed and resurrected:

"But as for me, I know that my Redeemer lives. In the end, he will stand upon the earth. After my skin is destroyed, then in my flesh shall I see God." —Job 19:25-26

Daniel, too, knew that he would be resurrected, because the angel who showed him visions concluded by telling him,

"'Go your way, Daniel, for the words are shut up and sealed until the time of the end. . . . But go your way till the end; and you shall rest, and shall stand in your allotted place at the end of the days.'" —Daniel 12:9-13 RSV

The prophet Isaiah wrote about the time when God will resurrect the dead and put an end to death itself:

"He has swallowed up death forever! The Lord Yahweh will wipe away tears from off all faces. . . . Your dead shall live. My dead bodies shall arise. Awake and sing, you who dwell in the dust; for your dew is like the dew of herbs, and the earth will cast forth the dead." —Isaiah 25:8; 26:19

But very little is revealed in the Old Testament about the condition of the dead in the meantime, prior to the resurrection. God left this information to be revealed through his Son. The Gospel message Jesus proclaimed revealed things that had previously been kept secret about death and about the way to eternal life:

"That it might be fulfilled which was spoken by the prophet, saying, I will open my mouth in parables; I will utter things which have been kept secret from the foundation of the world."

—Matthew 13:35 KJV

Much of the new information Jesus revealed touches on the afterlife—the heavenly reward awaiting his disciples and the punishment in store for the wicked. His calling sinners to repent, follow him, and gain immortality

"has now been revealed by the appearing of our Savior Jesus Christ, who has abolished death and brought life and immortality to light through the gospel" —2 Timothy 1:10 NKJV

Among Jesus' final words to his followers before he was arrested and taken from them, he spoke this assurance:

"'Let not your heart be troubled: ye believe in God, believe also in me. In my Father's house are many mansions: if it were not so, I would have told you. I go to prepare a place for you. And if I go and prepare a place for you, I will come again, and receive you unto myself; that where I am, there ye may be also.'"

—John 14:1-3 KJV

Besides comforting those who had followed him during his earthly ministry, Jesus went on to reveal that all future believers who would hear the Gospel and put faith in Christ will end up in heaven with him to behold his glory. After praying for his initial disciples, Jesus added these words:

"'My prayer is not for them alone. I pray also for those who will believe in me through their message . . . Father, I want those you have given me to be with me where I am, and to see my glory'"

—John 17:20-24 NIV

So, if we put faith in Jesus and follow him, we have the blessed assurance of everlasting life with him in heaven. Although there were hints of this hope in the Old Testament, Jesus revealed details of this hope that had been kept secret prior to his preaching. He revealed himself as the way to eternal life:

"Jesus saith unto him, I am the way, the truth, and the life: no man cometh unto the Father, but by me." —John 14:6 KJV

Jesus was the kindest, most loving man ever to walk the earth. He invited all of us to come to him, to receive perfect peace and rest:

"'Come unto me, all ye that labour and are heavy laden, and I will give you rest.'" —Matthew 11:28 KJV

Jesus' love drew people to him, wherever he went, even hardened prostitutes and macho soldiers. And he called everyone to repent and receive life.

But, besides revealing himself as the way to immortality, Jesus also said more about punishment after death than anyone else in the Bible.

"'And I say unto you my friends, Be not afraid of them that kill the body, and after that have no more that they can do. But I will forewarn you whom ye shall fear: Fear him, which after he hath killed hath power to cast into hell; yea, I say unto you, Fear him.'"

—Luke 12:4-5 KJV

Proclamation of the Gospel was 'Good News,' but it also made mankind more responsible in God's sight.

"In the past God overlooked such ignorance, but now he commands all people everywhere to repent. For he has set a day when he will judge the world with justice by the man he has appointed. He has given proof of this to all men by raising him from the dead." —Acts 17:30-31 NIV

This was indeed something new, both for the Gentiles who had been left largely without knowledge of the true God prior to this, and for the Jews who were being called from a distant organizational relationship with God the Father to come individually into a closer, more personal relationship through the Son.

Along with the call to repent from sin and follow Jesus, the Gospel message also revealed the consequences of rejecting this invitation—very serious consequences:

"If we deliberately keep on sinning after we have received the knowledge of the truth, no sacrifice for sins is left, but only a fearful expectation of judgment and of raging fire that will consume the enemies of God.

"Anyone who rejected the law of Moses died without mercy on the testimony of two or three witnesses. How much more severely do you think a man deserves to be punished who has trampled the Son of God under foot, who has treated as an unholy thing the blood of the covenant that sanctified him, and who has insulted the Spirit of grace? —Hebrews 10:26-29 NIV

So, the punishment for rejecting Christ is more severe than simply dying without mercy. This is, without doubt, a warning not to be ignored. Yet it should not leave any of us with an *unhealthy* fear of God—a fear that God might be cruel, unfair, unloving. Even those who know God personally, who feel his love, and who know that "God is love" (1 John 4:8), and who know that *he* is the one who teaches *us* to love—even we may fear for others. But to assure our hearts in this, he had recorded in his Word the fears that Abraham entertained when he heard of the punishment about to be inflicted on the city of Sodom.

God patiently put up with a lengthy cross-examination by Abraham, finally assuring him that the Judge of all the earth will indeed do what is right, what is fair, and what is good. (Compare Genesis 18:23-33)

If the thought of some receiving punishment after death troubles us, the solution does not lie in denying the Bible's inspiration, nor in explaining-away Jesus' words by distorting their meaning. Rather, the solution lies in *trusting* God. After all, that is what faith really means: not having God answer all of our questions, but putting our *trust* in God even in matters we find difficult to understand.

Jesus taught that childlike trust is required of us:

"'I tell you the truth, anyone who will not receive the kingdom of God like a little child will never enter it.'" —Luke 18:17 NIV

Instead of approaching the matter like scholars trying to understand God, we need to get down on our knees and take hold of his hand the way a little toddler trustingly holds onto his or her father's hand, securely confident that Dad has everything under control—that he will do the right thing and the loving thing.

Moreover, as we read Jesus' words on the subject of what happens after death, we need to attach significance, not only to what he says but also to what he leaves *unsaid.* Much of the controversy that has upset and divided sincere believers on these issues stems from human attempts to fill in the gaps—attempts to 'clarify' or 'clear up' the aspects that Jesus leaves 'unclear.' These human efforts range from highly intellectual theological essays, sprinkled with Greek words and other words that might as well be Greek to most readers, to works of fiction (Christian novels) that some today rely on for their theology, to works of art picturing horned red devils sticking pitchforks into tormented victims—all deviating from the impression one would receive by prayerfully reading the Bible itself.

Did it ever occur to such theological deep thinkers that Christ left certain matters unclear—full of annoying information gaps—because he *wanted* to, because he intended to? Although a parent sometimes tells a child, "If you leave the yard again, I'll send you to your room for the rest of the day," there are other times when a parent intentionally leaves the penalty for disobedience much less specific. "If you leave the yard again, you'll have to face your father when he comes home!" "If you leave the yard again, you'll wish you didn't!" So, can't we allow our heavenly Father to take the same approach?

Of course Jesus could have made it very clear what would happen to the dead—the good and the bad. If modern writers can spell it out clearly in black and white, as many indeed have done in books reflecting various opinions and interpretations, certainly the Author of the New Testament could have found the right words, too. He could have removed all ambiguities and spelled it all out. At the very least, he could have selected a chapter from one of the many books on the market today and canonized that chapter as part of inspired

116

Scripture. Then none of us would be left wondering exactly what happens to the dead. But, instead, God chose to leave certain questions unanswered or unclear—not so that our theologians can fill in the gaps for us, but rather so that we can trust in him, without knowing all the answers.

Another important consideration, often overlooked, is the fact that Jesus spoke to us in three different ways in Scripture:

(1) Literally, using what we could call 'straight talk.' He generally spoke this way to his disciples in private.

(2) In parables, or figurative stories with moral lessons. This is the way he often spoke to crowds of onlookers.

(3) Symbolically, in signs. This sort of presentation characterized the Apocalypse or book of Revelation.

Confusing Jesus' three forms of speech is a serious mistake, but one often made. If Jesus says that certain wicked men are put outside in the dark to weep and gnash their teeth, should we extrapolate this into a picture of children undergoing fiendish torture? If our sensibilities are offended by our concept of hell and who goes there, then perhaps our concept is wrong—even though we may have learned it from an authority figure with impressive credentials.

Just as some deny what the Bible says about punishment after death, there are other religious people who go overboard in the opposite direction, allowing their sadistic imagination to run wild as they picture devils with pitchforks having a grand time inflicting every brutal torture imaginable on helpless men, women, and children. This approach is every bit as unscriptural as other people's attempts to deny any punishment after death. Revelation 20:10 makes it plain that the devil himself is punished in the lake of fire—not placed in charge of an evil empire where he torments dead humans.

Where do the various twisted interpretations come from? Usually from religious authorities who claim the right to interpret the Bible for ignorant ordinary people. But, if you read the Gospels, you will note that Jesus spoke to *us*—to common people—not to professors, clergymen, doctors of theology, or any special class of Bible interpreters. If he intentionally bypassed the priests at Jerusalem's temple and the teachers in the synagogues, choosing instead to speak directly to fishermen, tax collectors, and prostitutes—how could we possibly think he meant for future generations to receive his words as interpreted and explained by some spiritual elite?

When today's dock worker, truck driver, housewife, or tax accountant picks up the Gospels and reads them, the impression they receive from Christ's words is the impression he meant for them to receive. If they subsequently change their minds and end up with a different impression after discussing and studying Scripture with so-called learned men, then that is more likely to be the wrong impression.

Jesus himself said,

"'I praise you, Father, Lord of heaven and earth, because you have hidden these things from the wise and learned, and revealed them to little children.'" —Matthew 11:25 NIV

Any human author can write with rarely-used words and complex sentence structure, so that only the well-educated reader will understand, but God did something much more difficult: He had his message presented in such a way that the well-educated reader would have no advantage; rather, the simple-minded reader with childlike trust would be the one more likely to grasp the message.

The chief obstacle to grasping what Jesus said about life after death is neither an inherent obscurity in his message, nor a deficiency in our own mental powers; rather, the greatest obstacle is the mass of twisted interpretations superimposed on his words by others. Encountering their interpretations before we encounter Jesus' words, we find ourselves approaching his words with numerous preconceived notions—seeing his words through tinted glasses, so to speak. The preceding discussion in this chapter is aimed principally at removing the colored glasses by untwisting some of those twisted interpretations. Still, as we read Jesus' words, we need to focus consciously on what he says, rather than on interpretations others have handed us.

With that in mind, the best way to learn what Jesus said about life after death is to prayerfully read the Gospels, and then go on to read the rest of the New Testament to see how Jesus' early disciples were inspired to explain and elaborate on his words. Rather than take my word for it, or accept some other author or speaker's interpretation of what Jesus taught, read it for yourself in the Bible.

'But my relatives won't like it
if I follow Jesus!'

'You don't want to become some kind of religious nut, do you?' 'Why don't you just stay in the church you were brought up in? It was good enough for us and our parents, so it should be good enough for you!' 'Okay, choose between Jesus and us, your family! You can't have both.' These are some of the things people hear from their relatives and loved ones when they choose to follow Jesus—the real Jesus of the Bible. And Jesus knew ahead of time that it would be like that for many of his followers. He said,

"'Don't think that I came to send peace on the earth. I didn't come to send peace, but a sword. For I came to set a man at odds against his father, and a daughter against her mother, and a daughter-in-law against her mother-in-law. A man's foes will be those of his own household. He who loves father or mother more than me is not worthy of me; and he who loves son or daughter more than me isn't worthy of me. He who doesn't take his cross and follow after me, isn't worthy of me.'" —Matthew 10:34-38

Jesus understood that his followers would face opposition from close relatives.

"Now great multitudes were going with him. He turned and said to them, 'If anyone comes to me, and doesn't disregard his own father, mother, wife, children, brothers, and sisters, yes, and his own life also, he can't be my disciple.

"'Whoever doesn't bear his own cross, and come after me, can't be my disciple. . . .

"'So therefore whoever of you who doesn't renounce all that he has, he can't be my disciple.'" —Luke 14:25-33

But there is a reward ahead for those who face such personal loss for the sake of following Jesus. He promised,

"'Everyone who has left houses, or brothers, or sisters, or father, or mother, or wife, or children, or lands, for my name's sake, will receive one hundred times, and will inherit eternal life.'"

—Matthew 19:29

Watching for Christ's return

After his death and resurrection, Jesus appeared alive to his followers over the course of some weeks. Then, as they watched, he rose into the sky until he disappeared from their sight. Two angels told Jesus' followers,

"'You men of Galilee, why do you stand looking into the sky? This Jesus, who was received up from you into the sky will come back in the same way as you saw him going into the sky.'" —Acts 1:11

Jesus himself spoke often to the disciples about his return, his second coming. It will not be like his humble birth in a barn or his submissive death on the cross. Rather, Jesus said he will return with great power and glory,

"'Then they will see the Son of Man coming in clouds with great power and glory. Then he will send out his angels, and will gather together his chosen ones from the four winds, from the ends of the earth to the ends of the sky.'" —Mark 13:26-27

Jesus will return as King of the kingdom of God. When he was put on trial before the high court of the Jews, and the high priest demanded to know whether Jesus was the Christ, the Son of God,

"Jesus said to him, 'You have said it. Nevertheless, I tell you, after this you will see the Son of Man sitting at the right hand of Power, and coming on the clouds of the sky.'" —Matthew 26:64

Jesus knew the Jewish religious leaders would understand this to be a reference to the book of Daniel, where the prophet wrote,

"I saw in the night visions, and behold, there came with the clouds of the sky one like a son of man, and he came even to the ancient of days, and they brought him near before him. There was given him dominion, and glory, and a kingdom, that all the peoples, nations, and languages should serve him: his dominion is an everlasting dominion, which shall not pass away, and his kingdom that which shall not be destroyed." —Daniel 7:13-14

Jesus devoted a significant portion of his teaching to the subject of his return. Many of his parables are devoted to this theme, describing how people would be caught by surprise, and would be rewarded or punished at that time. You may wish to read, for example, the parable of the ten virgins, the parable of the talents, and the parable of the sheep and the goats—all found in the twenty-fifth chapter of the Gospel of Matthew—and the parable of the faithful and wise servant at the end of the twenty-fourth chapter.

Jesus encouraged us to

"Therefore keep watch, because you do not know on what day your Lord will come.

. . . be ready, because the Son of Man will come at an hour when you do not expect him." —Matthew 24:42-44 NIV

We can "be ready" by living the way the Bible teaches us to live, and we can "keep watch" by eagerly praying for Christ's return and by paying attention to world events that point to the imminence of his coming. Which events? When Jesus told them about the coming destruction of the temple in Jerusalem, his disciples asked him, "Tell us, when will these things be? What is the sign of your coming, and of the end of the age?" (Matt. 24:3) Jesus answered them with a lengthy discussion of future world events, recorded for us in Matthew chapters 24-25, Mark chapter 13 and Luke chapter 21.

After speaking about armies surrounding and destroying Jerusalem, and the Jewish people being scattered worldwide, Jesus went on to speak of future events that would lead up to his return in power:

"There will be signs in the sun, moon, and stars; and on the earth anxiety of nations, in perplexity for the roaring of the sea and the waves; men fainting for fear, and for expectation of the things which are coming on the world: for the powers of the heavens will be shaken. Then they will see the Son of Man coming in a cloud with power and great glory. But when these things begin to happen, look up, and lift up your heads, because your redemption is near." —Luke 21:23-28

The Apostles also elaborated on the end times in their letters found in the New Testament. And the Old Testament prophets wrote at length on these matters, too.

It would take a whole book to discuss these prophecies adequately, and their relation to events down through history and in today's world. I have, in fact, addressed the end times prophecies in my book *LEFT BEHIND Answered Verse by Verse* and in the online version of that book that can be read for free at http://www.LeftBehindAnsweredVerseByVerse.com — as well as on my web sites http://www.BeastsOfRevelation.com http://www.JerusalemVerses.com http://www.BlueHelmetsToJerusalem.com http://www.1260days.com http://www.ProphecyTimeline.com http://www.BibleForetoldHolocaust.com http://www.WW7.com and http://www.TheGreatTribulation.net

There is considerable controversy among Christians as to how to interpret the various end times prophecies, and just how the foretold events will unfold. As was the case with those who were watching for the Jewish Messiah's appearing back in the first century, and who were surprised to see how Jesus fulfilled the messianic prophecies, we may all be surprised to see how the end times prophecies will actually be fulfilled, and when. But even a simple reading of the Bible gives those who are keeping watch good reason to believe that Jesus will return very soon.

We can learn, too, from God's past interventions in human affairs when mankind's behavior deteriorated to the point that God forcefully put a stop to it: the flood in Noah's day, the destruction of immoral Sodom and Gomorrah, and God's intervention to stop the construction of the tower of Babel. (See Genesis chapters 6-8, 11 and 18-19.) Has our world today reached the level of violence that prompted God to destroy the pre-flood world? Are people today behaving like the inhabitants of Sodom and Gomorrah? Has our technological advancement resulted in attitudes like those of the people who were building the tower of Babel? Then we have further reason to be in eager expectation of Christ's return.

Developments in the Middle East over the past few decades appear to have set the stage for prophesied events that could not take place without a Jewish Israel having been restored and a Jewish Jerusalem becoming powerful in the region. And without a United Nations organization and a restored Jewish Jerusalem, how could Zechariah's prophecy ever come true, that the nations of the earth will unite to attack?

"One day all the nations on earth will come together to attack Jerusalem. . . . I will bring all the nations together to fight Jerusalem. . . . Then the LORD will go to war against those nations." —Zechariah 12:3; 14:2-3 NCV

This appears to describe the same war as the battle of Armageddon foretold by the Apostle John in the book of Revelation:

"These evil spirits are the spirits of demons, which have power to do miracles. They go out to the kings of the whole world to gather them together for the battle on the great day of God Almighty. . . . to the place that is called Armageddon in the Hebrew language."

—Revelation 16:14-16 NCV

Could we imagine the United Nations mobilizing to enforce its resolutions concerning Jerusalem? That might well fit the scenario described by John and by Zechariah. There are various theories and interpretations circulating in the churches today as to just when and how Christ will return, and what will happen on earth as the day approaches. Will one of these theories prove to be correct? Or will Jesus surprise all of us? Only time will tell. Meanwhile, we need to follow Jesus' advice:

"'Take heed, watch and pray; for you do not know when the time is.'" —Mark 13:33 NKJV

How I Came to Follow Jesus

The Personal Testimony of David A. Reed

Figuring out what life is really all about, and coming to follow Jesus—the real Jesus—has been a long journey for me. My early religious training was in a big, white Unitarian church in rural New England, just south of Boston. I still remember the time when, in my boyish innocence, I expressed to the pastor my belief that God had actually parted the Red Sea to let Moses and the Israelites pass through; he turned to the assistant pastor and said, with a laugh, "This boy has a lot to learn." As I grew older I did, in fact, learn what this church taught. Encountering their pamphlet *What Unitarians Believe* , I read that "Some Unitarians believe in God, and some do not"—and quickly realized the ministers must have been among those who did not believe.

By the time I was fourteen years old, I had reached my own conclusion that religion was "the opium of the people," a convenient thought for an adolescent who preferred not to have God watching him all the time. And when I went on to Harvard University, I found that atheism and agnosticism flourished there, too. So, between the Unitarian Church and my Ivy League schooling, I seldom encountered any strong pressure to believe in God.

By the time I was twenty-two, though, I had thought through atheistic evolution to it its ultimate end: a pointless existence, followed by death. After all, if humans were nothing more than the last in a series of chemical and biological accidents, then any 'meaning' or 'purpose' we might try to find in life would just be a self-deceptive fiction produced in our own minds. It would have no real connection with the harsh, cold reality of a universe where nothing really mattered. So, I saw myself faced with two choices: God or suicide. Since suicide would be an easy way out for me—I believed there was nothing after death—but would leave those who cared about me to face the pain I would cause, I began to think about God.

Coincidentally (perhaps?), a Jehovah's Witness was assigned to work alongside me at my job. Since God was on my mind, I began asking him questions about his beliefs. His answers amazed me. It was the first time that I had ever heard religious thoughts presented in a tight-knit logical framework. Everything that he said fit together. He had an answer for every question, and so I kept coming up with more questions. Before long, he was conducting a study with me twice a week in the Watchtower Society's new (1968) book *The Truth That Leads to Eternal Life*.

In no time, I became a very zealous Witness. After receiving my initial indoctrination and getting baptized, I served as a full-time 'pioneer minister.' This required that I spend at least one hundred hours each month preaching from house to house and conducting home Bible studies—actually a commitment of much more than a hundred hours, since travel time could not be included in my monthly 'field service report.' I kept on 'pioneering' until 1971, when I married Penni, who had been raised in the organization and who also 'pioneered.'

My zeal for Jehovah and my proficiency in preaching were rewarded, after a few years, with appointment as an elder. In that capacity I taught the 150-odd people in my home congregation on a regular basis, and made frequent visits to other congregations as a Sunday morning speaker. Occasionally, I also received assignments to speak to audiences ranging in the thousands at Jehovah's Witness assemblies.

Other responsibilities I cared for included presiding over the other local elders, handling correspondence between the local congregation and the Society's Brooklyn headquarters, and serving on judicial committees set up to deal with cases of wrongdoing in the congregation. (I can recall disfellowshipping people for such offenses as selling drugs at Kingdom Hall, smoking cigarettes, wife-swapping, and having a Christmas decoration in the home.)

Although we were not able to continue 'pioneering' after our marriage, Penni and I remained very zealous for the preaching work. Between the two of us, we conducted 'home Bible studies' with dozens of people, and brought well over twenty of them into the organization as baptized Jehovah's Witnesses. We also put 'the Kingdom' first in our personal lives by keeping our secular employment to a minimum and living in an inexpensive three-room apartment in order to be able to devote more time to the door-to-door preaching activity.

What interrupted this life of full dedication to the Watchtower organization, and caused us to enter a path that would lead us out? In one word, it was *Jesus* . Let me explain:

When Penni and I were at a large Witness convention, we saw a handful of opposers picketing outside. One of them carried a sign that said, "READ THE BIBLE, NOT THE WATCHTOWER." We had no sympathy for the picketers, but we did feel convicted by this sign, because we knew that we had been reading Watchtower publications to the exclusion of reading the Bible. (Later on, we actually counted up all of the material that the organization expected Witnesses to read. The books, magazines, lessons, etc. added up to over three thousand pages each year, compared with less than two hundred pages of Bible reading assigned—and most of that was in the Old Testament.

The majority of Witnesses were so bogged down by the three thousand pages of the organization's literature that they never got around to doing the Bible reading.)

After seeing the picket sign Penni turned to me and said, "We should be reading the Bible **and** *The Watchtower.*" I agreed; so, we began doing regular personal Bible reading.

That's when we began to think about Jesus. Not that we began to question the Watchtower's teaching that Christ was just Michael the archangel in human flesh—It didn't even occur to us to question that. But we were really impressed with Jesus as a person: what he said and did, how he treated people. We wanted to be his followers. Especially, we were struck with how Jesus responded to the hypocritical religious leaders of the day, the Scribes and Pharisees. I remember reading, over and over again, the accounts relating how the Pharisees objected to Jesus' healing on the Sabbath, his disciples' eating with unwashed hands, and other details of behavior that violated their traditions. How I loved Jesus' response: "You hypocrites, Isaiah aptly prophesied about you, when he said, 'This people honors me with their lips, yet their heart is far removed from me. It is in vain that they keep worshiping me, because they teach commands of men as doctrines.'" (Matt. 15:7-9 the JWs' *New World Translation*)

Commands of men as doctrines! That thought stuck in my mind. And I began to realize that, in fulfilling my role as an elder, I was acting more like a Pharisee than a follower of Jesus. I was teaching commands of men as doctrines. For example, the elders were the enforcers of all sorts of petty rules about dress and grooming. We told 'sisters' how long they could wear their dresses, and we told 'brothers' how to comb their hair, how to trim their sideburns, and what sort of flare or taper they could wear in their pants. We actually told people that they could not please God unless they conformed. It reminded me of the Pharisees who condemned Jesus' disciples for eating with unwashed hands.

My own dress and grooming conformed to the letter. But I ran into problems with newly interested young men that I brought to Kingdom Hall. Instead of telling them to buy a white shirt and sport coat, and to cut their hair short, I now told them, "Don't be disturbed if people at Kingdom Hall dress and groom a little on the old-fashioned side. You can continue as you are. God doesn't judge people by their haircut or their clothing." But that didn't work. Someone else would tell them to get a haircut, or offer to give them a white shirt—or they would simply feel so out of place that they left never to return.

This upset me, because I believed their life depended on joining 'God's organization.' If we Witnesses acted like Pharisees to the point of driving young people away from the only way to salvation, their innocent blood would be on our hands. Talking to the other elders about it didn't help. They felt that the old styles were inherently righteous. But then Jesus' example came to mind:

"And he went on from there and entered their synagogue. And behold, there was a man with a withered hand. And they asked him, 'Is it lawful to heal on the sabbath?' so that they might accuse him. He said to them, 'What man of you, if he has one sheep and it falls into a pit on the sabbath, will not lay hold of it and lift it out? Of how much more value is a man than a sheep! So it is lawful to do good on the sabbath.' Then he said to the man, 'Stretch out your hand.'" (Matt. 12:9-13 RSV)

If I were truly to follow Jesus, instead of men, I saw only one course open to me. I personally violated the tradition of the elders by letting my hair grow a half inch over my ears. My reasoning was: How can they pressure a newcomer to get a haircut, now, with one of the elders wearing the same style?

Well, the other elders reacted the same way the Pharisees did when Jesus told the man to stretch out his hand. Scripture says they "went out and took counsel against him, how to destroy him." (Matt. 12:14 RSV) It took them a while to react, but the elders actually put me on trial, called in witnesses to testify, and spent dozens of hours discussing half an inch of hair.

Grooming was not the real issue, however. For me it was a question of whose disciple I was. Was I a follower of Jesus, or an obedient servant to a human hierarchy? The elders who put me on trial knew that that was the real issue, too. They kept asking, "Do you believe that the Watchtower Society is God's organization? Do you believe that the Society speaks as Jehovah's mouthpiece?" At that time I answered *Yes* because I still did believe it was God's organization—but that it had become corrupt, like the Jewish religious system at the time when Jesus was opposed by the Pharisees.

It was what I said at the congregation meetings that got me into real trouble, though. I was still an elder, so, when I was assigned to give a 15-minute talk on the book of Zechariah at the Thursday night 'Theocratic Ministry School' meeting, I took advantage of the opportunity to encourage the audience to read the Bible. In fact, I told them that, if their time was limited and they had to choose between reading the Bible and reading *The Watchtower* magazine, they should choose the Bible, because it was inspired by God while *The Watchtower* was not inspired and often taught errors that had to be corrected later.

Not surprisingly, that was the last time they allowed me to give a talk. But I could still speak from my seat during question-and-answer periods at the meetings. Everyone was expected to answer in their own words, but not in their own thoughts. You were to give the thought found in the paragraph of the lesson being discussed. But, after I said a few things they didn't like, they stopped giving me the microphone.

With the new perspective that I was gaining from Bible reading, it upset me to see the organization elevate itself above Scripture, as it did when the December 1, 1981, *Watchtower* said: "Jehovah God has also provided his visible organization . . . Unless we are in touch with this channel of communication that God is using, we will not progress along the road to life, no matter how much Bible reading we do." (page 27, ¶ 4) It really disturbed me to see those men elevate themselves above God's Word. Since I could not speak out at the meetings, I decided to try writing.

That's when I started publishing the newsletter *Comments from the Friends*. I wrote articles questioning what the organization was teaching, and signed them with the pen name 'Bill Tyndale, Jr.'—a reference to sixteenth century English Bible translator William Tyndale, who was burned at the stake for what he wrote. To avoid getting caught, Penni and I drove across the state line at night to an out-of-state post office and mailed the articles in unmarked envelopes. We sent them to local Witnesses and also to hundreds of Kingdom Halls all across the country, whose addresses we had obtained from telephone books at the town library.

Penni and I knew that we had to leave the Jehovah's Witnesses. But, to us, it was similar to the question of what to do in a burning apartment building. Do you escape through the nearest exit? Or, do you bang on doors first, waking the neighbors and helping them escape, too? We felt an obligation to help others get out—especially our families and our 'students' that we had brought into the organization. If we had just walked out, our families left behind would have been forbidden to associate with us.

But, after a few weeks a friend discovered that I was the publisher of the newsletter and turned me in. So, one night when Penni and I were returning home from conducting a Bible study, two elders stepped out of a parked car, accosted us in the street, and questioned us about the newsletter. They wanted to put us on trial for publishing it, but we simply stopped going to the Kingdom Hall. By that time most of our former friends there had become quite hostile toward us. One young man called on the phone and threatened to "come over and take care of" me if he got another one of our newsletters. And another Witness actually left a couple of death threats on our answering machine. The elders went ahead and tried us *in absentia* and disfellowshipped us.

This meant that other JWs—including our close friends—were now forbidden to speak to us, even to say hello if they passed us on the street. If they chose to associate with us, they too would face disfellowshipping. It was as if everyone we knew had died. This was an especially painful time for Penni. But we had our new friend Jesus. We identified with Paul, who wrote, "I count all things to be loss in view of the surpassing value of knowing Christ Jesus my Lord, for whom I have suffered the loss of all things, and count them but rubbish so that I may gain Christ." (Phil. 3:8 NASB)

It was a great relief to be out from under the oppressive yoke of that organization. But, we now had to face the immediate challenge of where to go and what to believe. It takes some time to re-think your entire religious outlook on life. Before leaving the Watchtower, we had rejected the claims that the organization was God's 'channel of communication,' that Christ returned invisibly in the year 1914, and that the 'great crowd' of believers since 1935 should not partake of the communion loaf and cup. But, we were only beginning to re-examine other doctrines. And we had not yet come into fellowship with Christians outside the JW organization.

All Penni and I knew was that we wanted to follow Jesus and that the Bible contained all the information we needed. So, we really devoted ourselves to reading the Bible, and to prayer. We also invited our families and remaining friends to meet in our apartment on Sunday mornings. While the Witnesses gathered at Kingdom Hall to hear a lecture and study *The Watchtower*, we met to read the Bible. As many as fifteen attended—mostly family, but some friends also.

We were just amazed at what we found in prayerfully reading the New Testament over and over again—things that we had never appreciated before, like the closeness that the early disciples had with the risen Lord, the activity of the Holy Spirit in the early church, and Jesus' words about being 'born again.'

All those years as Jehovah's Witnesses, the Watchtower had taken us on a guided tour through the Bible. We gained a lot of knowledge about the Old Testament, and we could quote a lot of Scripture, but we never heard the Gospel of salvation in Christ. We never learned to depend on Jesus for our salvation and to look to him personally as our Lord. Everything centered around the Watchtower's works program, and people were expected to come to Jehovah God through the organization.

When I realized from reading Romans, chapter 8, and John, chapter 3, that I needed to be 'born of the Spirit,' I was afraid at first. Jehovah's Witnesses believe that some 'born again' people, who claim to have the Holy Spirit, are actually possessed by demons. And so I feared that, if I prayed out loud to turn my life over to Jesus Christ, some demon might be listening; and the demon might jump in and possess me, pretending to be the Holy Spirit. (Many Jehovah's Witnesses live in constant fear of the demons. Some of our friends would even throw out second-hand furniture and clothing, fearing that demons could enter their homes through such articles.) But, then I read Jesus' words at Luke 11:9-13. In a context where he was teaching about prayer and casting out unclean spirits, Jesus said: "And I say to you, ask, and it will be given to you; seek, and you will find; knock, and it will be opened to you. For everyone who asks receives, and he who seeks finds, and to him who knocks it will be opened. If a son asks for bread from any of you who is a father, will he give him a stone? Or if he asks for a fish, will he give him a serpent instead of a fish? Or if he asks for an egg, will he offer him a scorpion? If you then, being evil, know how to give good gifts to your children, how much more will your heavenly Father give the Holy Spirit to those who ask Him!" (NKJV)

I knew, after reading those words, that I could safely ask for Christ's Spirit (Rom. 8:9), without fearing that I would receive a demon. So, in the early morning privacy of our kitchen, I proceeded to confess my need for salvation and to commit my life to Christ.

About a half hour later, I was on my way to work, and I was about to pray again. It had been my custom for many years to start out my prayers by saying, 'Jehovah God, . . .' But, this time when I opened my mouth to pray, I started out by saying, 'Father, . . .' It was not because I had reasoned on the subject and reached the conclusion that I should address God differently; the word *Father* just came out, without my even thinking about it. Immediately, I understood why: 'God has sent forth the Spirit of His Son into your hearts, crying out, "*Abba* , Father!"' (Galatians 4:6 NKJV) I wept with joy at God's confirmation of this new, more intimate relationship with him.

When I returned home that evening and sat down at the dinner table, it occurred to me as I was about to pray before our meal that I had always been in the habit of beginning my prayer by addressing "Jehovah God," as the Watchtower Society had taught us. How would I explain to Penni that I now addressed God as "Father"? But, to my surprise, just as I opened my mouth to pray, Penni interrupted me and said, "You know, David, we should really be calling God 'Father' when we pray."

Penni and I soon developed the desire to worship and praise the Lord in a congregation of believers, and to benefit from the wisdom of mature Christians. Since the small group of ex-JWs was still meeting in our apartment on Sunday mornings for Bible reading, and most of them were not yet ready to venture into a church, we began visiting churches that had evening services. One church we attended was so legalistic that we almost felt as though we were back in the Kingdom Hall. Another was so liberal that the sermon always seemed to be on philosophy or politics—instead of Jesus. Finally, though, the Lord led us to a congregation where we felt comfortable, and where the focus was on Jesus Christ and his Gospel, rather than on side issues. And, desiring to be obedient to Jesus' command to "make disciples of all nations, baptizing them in the name of the Father and of the Son and of the Holy Spirit," (Matthew 28:19 NIV), Penni and I received Christian baptism.

Penni went on to teach Fifth Grade in a Christian school that had students from about seventeen different churches. She really enjoyed it, because she could tie in the Scriptures with all sorts of subjects. For some eighteen years I continued publishing *Comments from the Friends* as a quarterly newsletter aimed at reaching Jehovah's Witnesses with the Gospel, and helping Christians interested in talking to JWs. It also contained articles of special interest to ex-Witnesses. Subscribers were found in a dozen foreign countries, as well as all across the United States and Canada. Many back issues are still available in web format at http://www.CFTF.com. I have also written a number of books on Jehovah's Witnesses, on Mormonism (with an ex-Mormon co-author), on end-times prophecies, and on other Bible topics. My web sites encourage Bible reading and belief in the Bible as God's unfailing inspired Word. Besides continuing to write, I speak occasionally to church groups on these matters.

The thrust of my outreach ministry is to help people break free from deception and put faith in the original Gospel of Christ as it is presented in the Bible. The most important lesson Penni and I learned since leaving the Jehovah's Witnesses is that Jesus is not just a historical figure that we read about. He is alive and is actively involved with Christians today, just as he was back in the first century. He personally saves us, teaches us, and leads us. This personal relationship with God through his Son Jesus Christ is so wonderful! The individual who knows Jesus and follows him will not even think about following anyone else: "A stranger they will not follow, but they will flee from him, for they do not know the voice of strangers. . . . My sheep hear my voice, and I know them, and they follow me; and I give them eternal life, and they shall never perish, and no one shall snatch them out of my hand." (John 10:5,27-28 RSV)

Why this book?

Our dear friend Katy Tripp gave my wife a handful of booklets, brochures pamphlets and tracts, and urged her to, 'Ask David to write a book like this.' Each of the items was a brief introduction to Christianity, presenting the basic Gospel message in simple terms to non-believers or new believers.

The need for such a book struck me, although there are churches on every street corner, and there are already many books introducing Christianity or admonishing new believers. Why would another such book be needed now?

Because, in today's world we find many confused, distorted and watered-down teachings as to what it means to be a follower of Jesus.

People are often urged to 'receive Christ' or to 'accept Jesus Christ as Lord and Savior' without being given a biblical understanding of what that means and involves. It is popular today to stress Jesus' role as the Savior who forgives, without spelling out his role as the Lord whom we must obey.

The Gospels show that Jesus started out his preaching ministry with a call to repent: "... Jesus began to preach, and to say, 'Repent! ...'" (Matthew 4:17), and that he concluded it with the same message: "that repentance and remission of sins should be preached in his name to all the nations ..." (Luke 24:47) (The meaning of *repent* is to feel sorry for past conduct, to regret or be conscience-stricken about past actions, attitudes, etc.—with such sorrow as to want to change one's life for the better.)

Jesus' disciples were faithful to the commission he gave them, and preached repentance. Peter urged his first public audience to "Repent, and be baptized" (Acts 2:38) Paul told a pagan audience that, "The times of ignorance therefore God overlooked. But now he commands that all people everywhere should repent." (Acts 17:30) Later, Paul summed up his ministry by explaining that he "declared first to them of Damascus, at Jerusalem, and throughout all the country of Judea, and also to the Gentiles, that they should repent and turn to God, doing works worthy of repentance." (Acts 26:20)

The call in Scripture to repent, and to do works worthy of repentance, is not given just to non-believers, but is also repeated to the members of Christian churches. In the opening chapters of Revelation, the risen Christ addressed messages to seven prominent Christian churches in Asia Minor. To one of those churches, Jesus said, "... repent and do the first works; or else ..." (Rev. 2:5) To another church he said, "I have a few things against you, because you have there some who hold the teaching of Balaam ... you also have some who hold to the teaching of the Nicolaitans likewise. Repent therefore, or else ..." (Rev. 2:14-16)

To yet another of these seven churches, the risen Christ said, ". . . I have this against you, that you tolerate your woman, Jezebel, who calls herself a prophetess. She teaches and seduces my servants to commit sexual immorality, and to eat things sacrificed to idols. I gave her time to repent, but she refuses to repent of her sexual immorality. Behold, I will throw her into a bed, and those who commit adultery with her into great oppression, unless they repent of her works. I will kill her children with Death, and all the assemblies will know that I am he who searches the minds and hearts. I will give to each one of you according to your deeds." (Rev 2:20-23) Could that same message apply to some churches today?

To another of those first century churches, Jesus said, ". . . I know your works, that you have a reputation of being alive, but you are dead. Wake up, and keep the things that remain, which you were about to throw away, for I have found no works of yours perfected before my God. Remember therefore how you have received and heard. Keep it, and repent. If therefore you won't watch, I will come as a thief, and you won't know what hour I will come upon you." (Rev. 3:1-3)

Jesus had strong words for five of the seven churches. Only two escaped receiving such warnings and calls to repent.

Are today's churches in better shape than those seven churches? Or in worse shape? Might we find five out of seven churches today in line for condemnation rather than praise? The condition of the churches highlights the need for each individual to look to Jesus and to the Scriptures for direction, rather than just passively listen to the preaching from the church pulpit. My aim in this book is to help the reader do that.

There is a need for this because today's churches are filled with false teachers who omit the call to repent, and who present Jesus as Savior without teaching that we must obey Jesus as Lord. They justify this false teaching by dismissing our acts of obedience as 'works' that are not required, since we are saved by 'faith.'

The balance between 'faith' and 'works' was a controversial issue in the early Church, but for a different reason. The Apostles had to warn the congregations they wrote to against false teachers who wanted to require Christian converts to be circumcised as Jews and to keep the law of Moses. In reply to them, Paul countered their false teaching by explaining that "a man is not justified by the works of the law but through faith in Jesus Christ" (Galatians 2:16) and that "by the works of the law, no flesh will be justified . . ." (Romans 3:20) But some false teachers today go off in the opposite direction and use such passages to 'prove' that Christianity is all about faith, and that our works don't matter much at all. They present this twisted teaching by focusing on certain passages while omitting or explaining away other passages of Scripture. But a balanced reading of the whole New Testament reveals that both faith and works are key elements of following Jesus.

As Paul himself said, converts are expected to "repent and turn to God, doing works worthy of repentance." (Acts 26:20) In his book *The Cost of Discipleship*, German Theologian Dietrich Bonhoeffer condemned "the preaching of forgiveness without requiring repentance" as "cheap grace." Such "cheap grace" is not the message Jesus preached. As Paul explained, ". . . by grace you have been saved through faith, and that not of yourselves; it is the gift of God, not of works, that no one would boast. For we are his workmanship, created in Christ Jesus for good works, which God prepared before that we would walk in them." (Ephesians 2:8-10) In other words, we are saved by faith so that we can go on to do good works. Our good behavior demonstrates that we have repented of our sins.

So, how would this book be different from others with a similar theme? I resolved to present the invitation to "Come, follow Jesus!" in strictly biblical terms, by quoting biblical passages at length and by presenting them with just a minimum of additional comment or discussion.

After all, it is in the Bible that we find Jesus inviting us to follow him. And along with that invitation, he spells out how we should go about doing so. "Jesus came to them and spoke to them, saying, 'All authority has been given to me in heaven and on earth. Go, and make disciples of all nations, baptizing them in the name of the Father and of the Son and of the Holy Spirit, teaching them to observe all things that I commanded you. Behold, I am with you always, even to the end of the age.'" (Matthew 28:18-20)

So, followers of Jesus must learn to "observe all things that I commanded you." Otherwise, they would face this rebuke: "Why do you call me, 'Lord, Lord,' and don't do the things which I say?" (Luke 6:46) And where else can we find those things that Jesus commanded, but in the pages of the Gospels of Matthew, Mark, Luke and John where Jesus' words are recorded? And if any interpretation of those words may be needed, we find that interpretation in the Acts of the Apostles, as well as in the New Testament letters of Peter, Paul, James, John and Jude.

Today, however, there are many, many different interpretations of what "following Jesus" consists of, and how a new believer should go about accepting Christ's invitation.

For some it is a matter of joining a particular organization or institutional church, perhaps even with the stern warning that there is no salvation outside of that organization. (My own experience with the Jehovah's Witness sect was like that, but there are many, many other sects and more traditional churches that take a similar approach.) For others, "following Jesus" involves adopting a particular code of ethics, or joining a program of social action. For still others, it is a matter of adopting a particular theology, perhaps as a follower of a certain noteworthy theologian, teacher or church leader, living or long dead.

For the adherents of such views it is inconceivable that someone might simply read the Bible, fall on his or her knees in prayer, and become a follower of Jesus. It would also be necessary to join their organization, or follow their program, or study and adopt their theology, and so on.

Certain cults and even some more reputable churches teach that the Bible can be properly understood only within the framework of their program of instruction. And their instruction often consists of what I call "scripture sandwiches"—a Bible verse or two sandwiched between the author's or speaker's discussion, followed by another verse or two later on, again sandwiched between someone's interpretation or application. There is nothing wrong with a certain amount of that sort of teaching, but we also need to feed on the Word itself. A steady diet of scripture sandwiches is not healthful. In such sandwiches, not only is the biblical context omitted, but the verses are actually placed in a different context, namely the context of the sermon or book.

To grasp how this can change the meaning, think of a complete biblical passage (perhaps a full chapter or two) as a cooked turkey breast. Someone cutting into that turkey breast and eating it will know what it tastes like. However, someone who is given just a thin slice smothered with mustard between layers of rye bread will know only what the sandwich tastes like—not the taste of the turkey itself.

Similarly, the original flavor or meaning of a Bible verse can be completely lost or changed when sandwiched between introductory words and concluding applications in the pages of someone's book or sermon.

Feeding on steady diet of such "scripture sandwiches," some churchgoers never really come to know the Bible. But they do learn their leader's teachings, along with the proof texts their teacher uses to make those teachings appear to be "Bible-based."

In contrast to that approach, I agree with the Apostle Paul who told Timothy, "From infancy, you have known the holy Scriptures which are able to make you wise for salvation through faith, which is in Christ Jesus. Every Scripture is God-breathed and profitable for teaching, for reproof, for correction, and for instruction in righteousness, that the man of God may be complete, thoroughly equipped for every good work." (2 Timothy 3:15-17) I believe that Scripture is the essential guide for those who would follow Christ. So, I have attempted here in this book to provide excerpts from Scripture to whet the appetite of those who "hunger and thirst after righteousness." (Matthew 5:6) My hope is that those who read this book will go on to read the Bible itself—not just once but over and over again, learning more and drawing closer to God with each prayerful reading.

Reading the Bible is essential. But it is not sufficient to be mere readers or hearers of the word. As James wrote, "But be doers of the word, and not only hearers, deluding your own selves." (James 1:22) Receptive hearts will believe what they read in the New Testament, and will respond by embracing Christ himself. What a mistake it would be to imitate those who constantly study Scripture but miss this point. Jesus said to some students of the Bible, "You search the Scriptures, because you think that in them you have eternal life; and these are they which testify about me. Yet you will not come to me, that you may have life." (John 5:39-40)

Scripture comes alive for us when we come to Jesus personally, as he invites us.

So, I produced this book to invite you, the reader, to meet Jesus Christ. You can do this through prayer, and through prayerfully reading the written Word of God. Jesus promises to respond by receiving you, by revealing himself to you, and by coming to live with you. He says:

"'Come to me, all you who labor and are heavily burdened, and I will give you rest. Take my yoke upon you, and learn from me, for I am gentle and lowly in heart; and you will find rest for your souls. For my yoke is easy, and my burden is light." (Matthew 11:28-30) "He who comes to me I will in no way throw out." (John 6:37) "My sheep hear my voice, and I know them, and they follow me. I give eternal life to them. They will never perish, and no one will snatch them out of my hand." (John 10:27-28) "One who has my commandments, and keeps them, that person is one who loves me. One who loves me will be loved by my Father, and I will love him, and will reveal myself to him. . . . If a man loves me, he will keep my word. My Father will love him, and we will come to him, and make our home with him.'"—John 14:21, 23

Jesus says:

"Come, follow me."

—Luke 18:22

9738838R0008

Made in the USA
Charleston, SC
08 October 2011